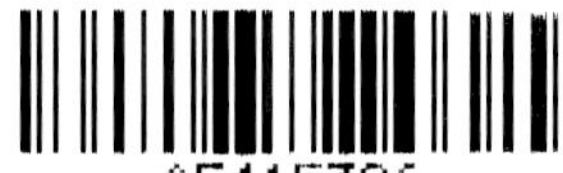
AF415396

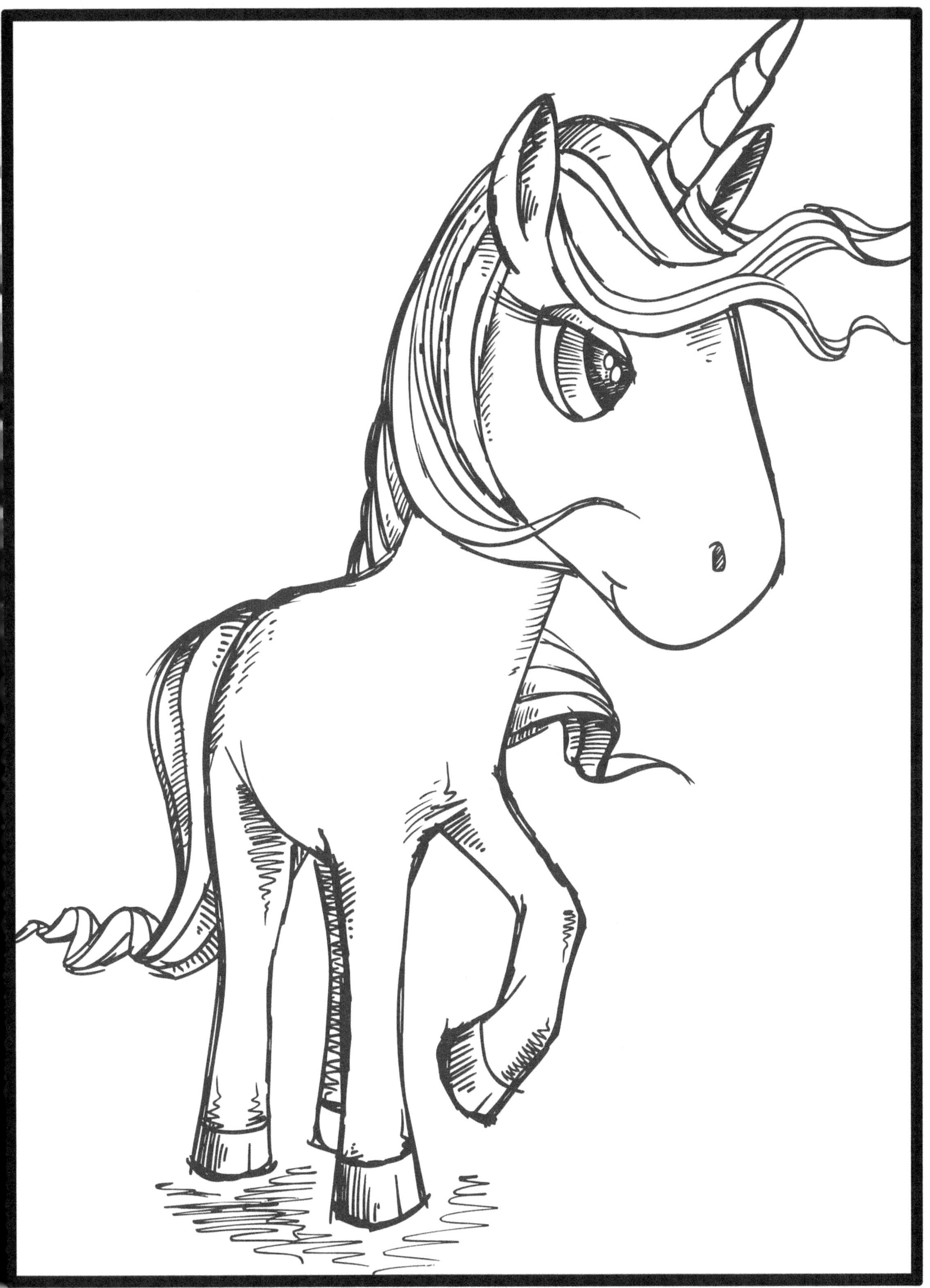

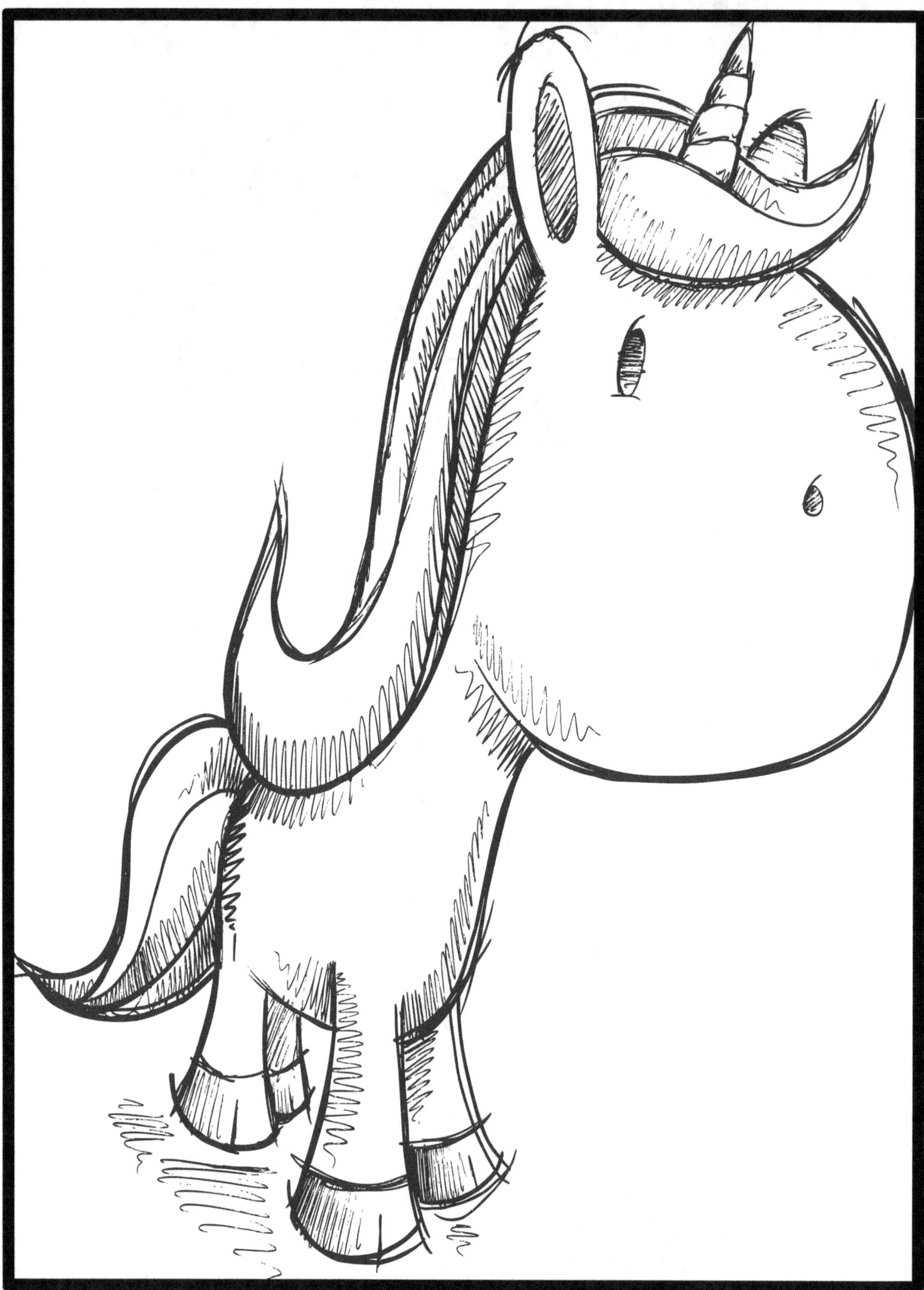

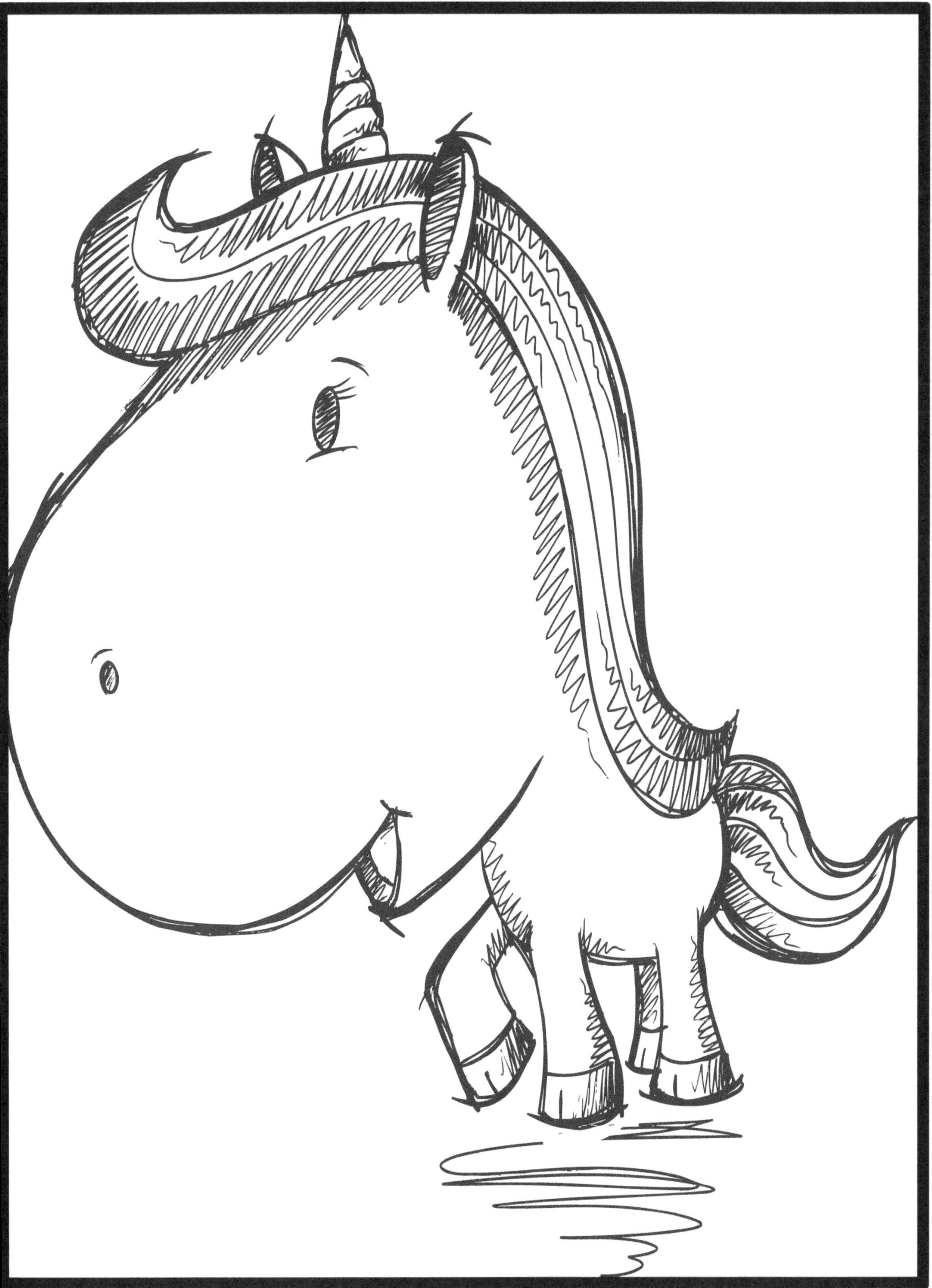

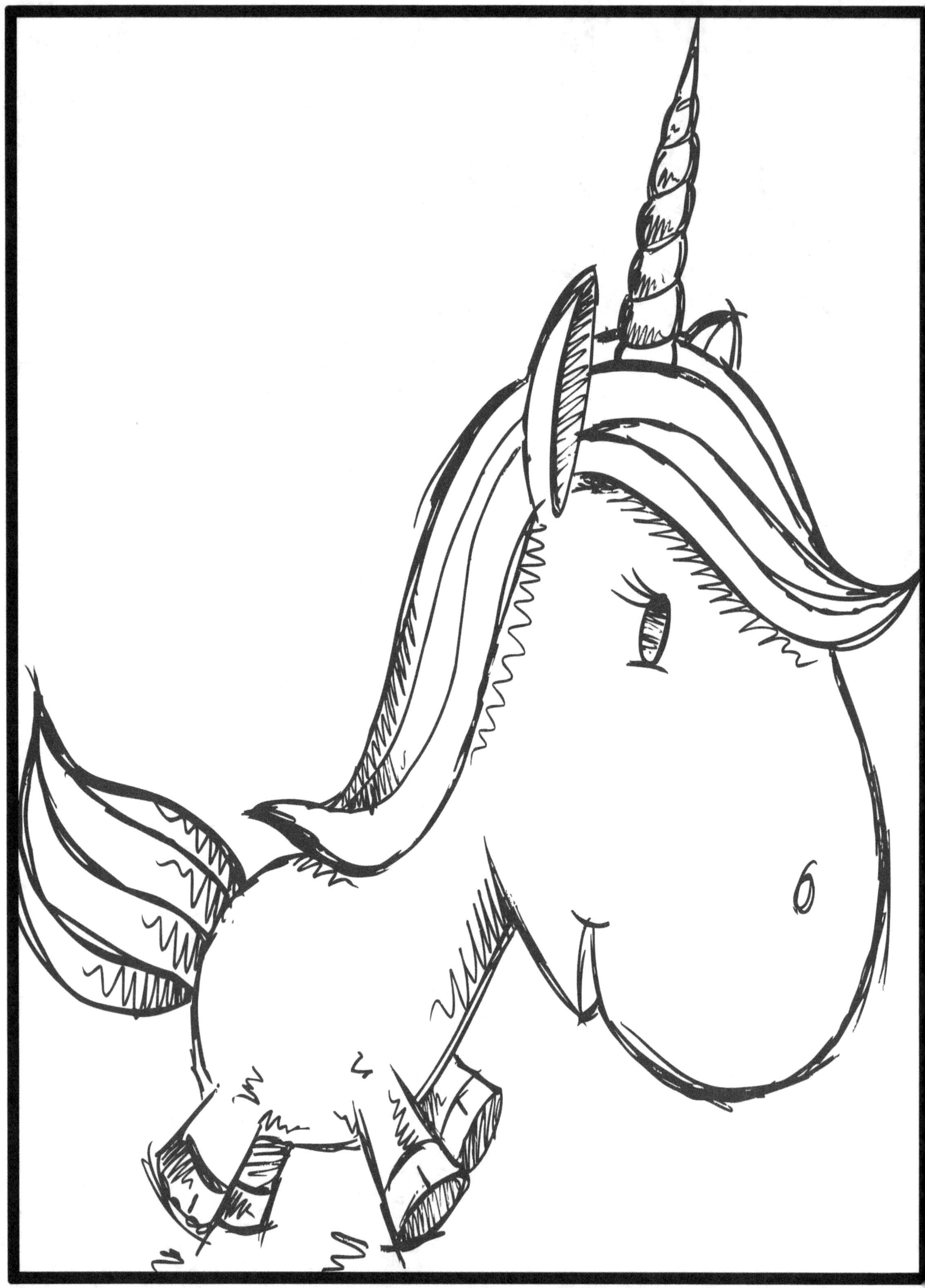

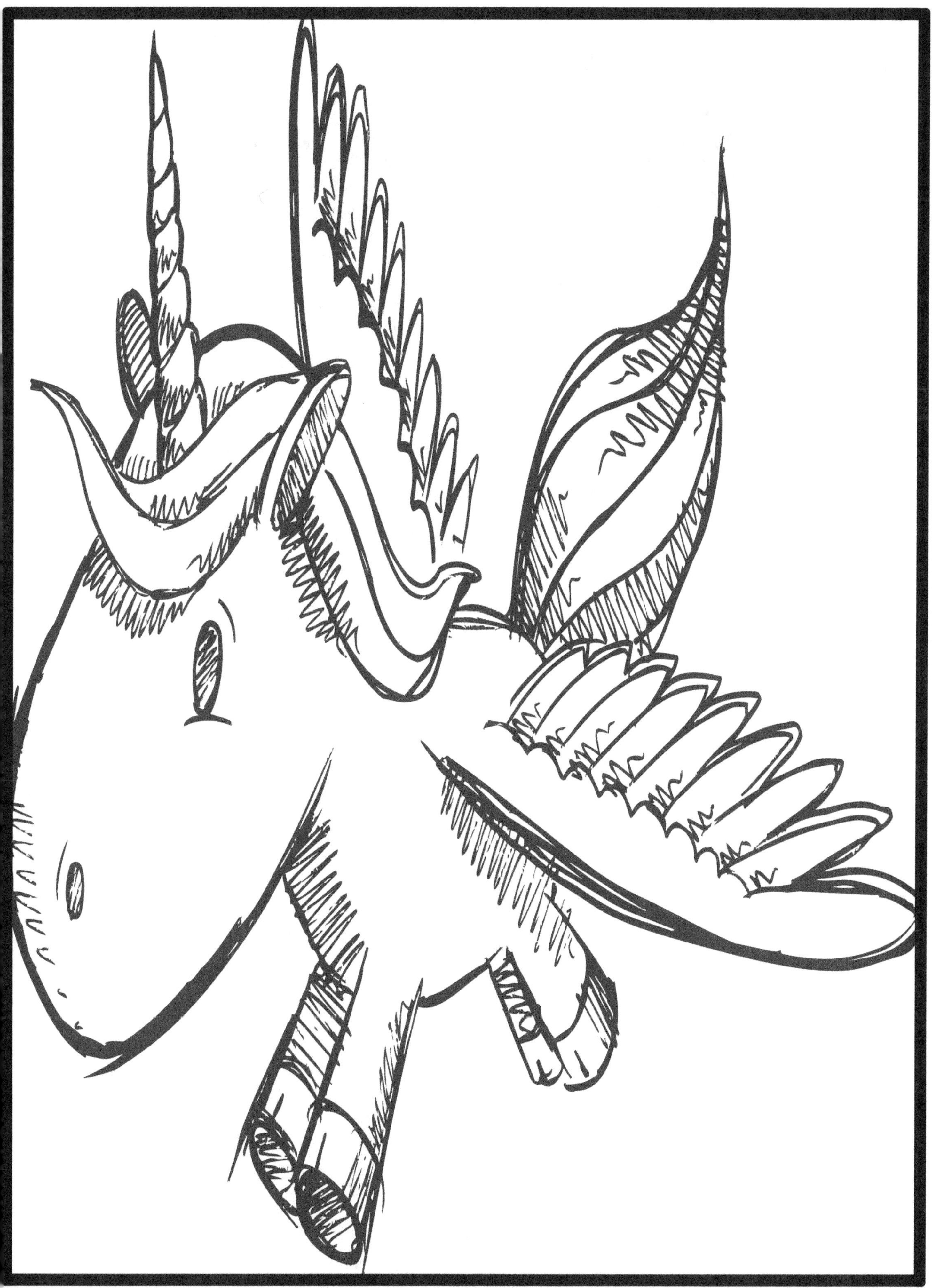

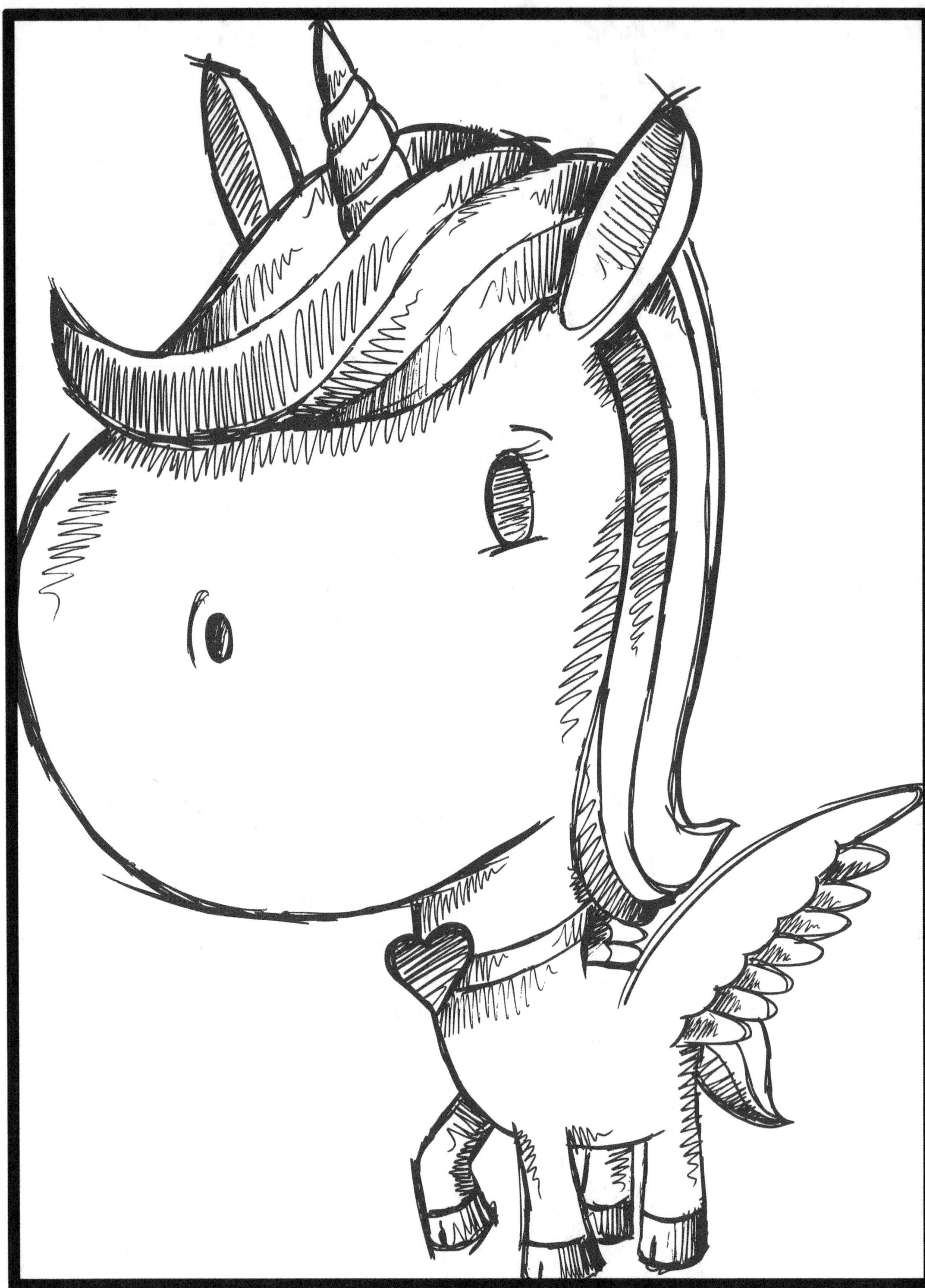

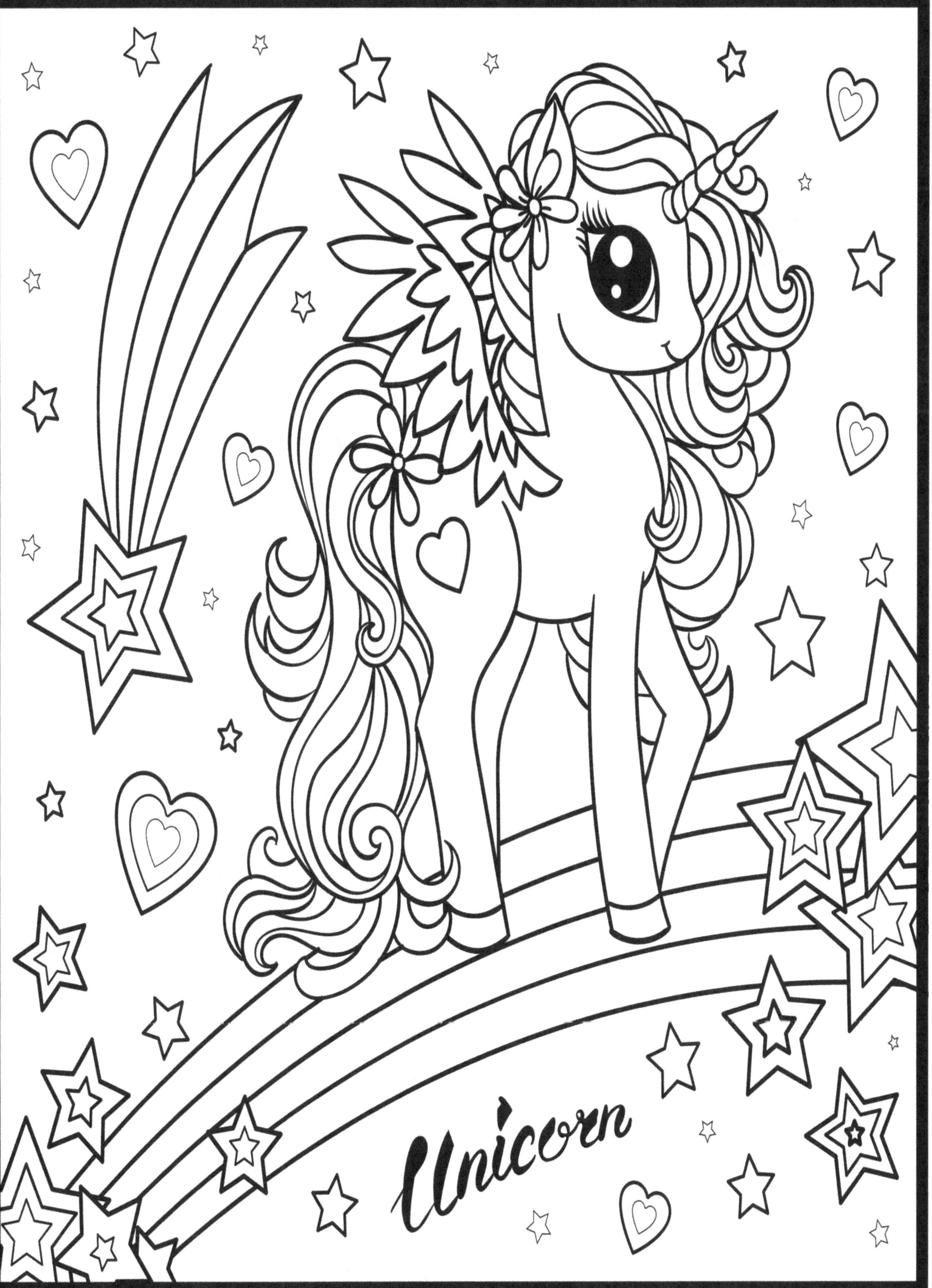
Unicorn

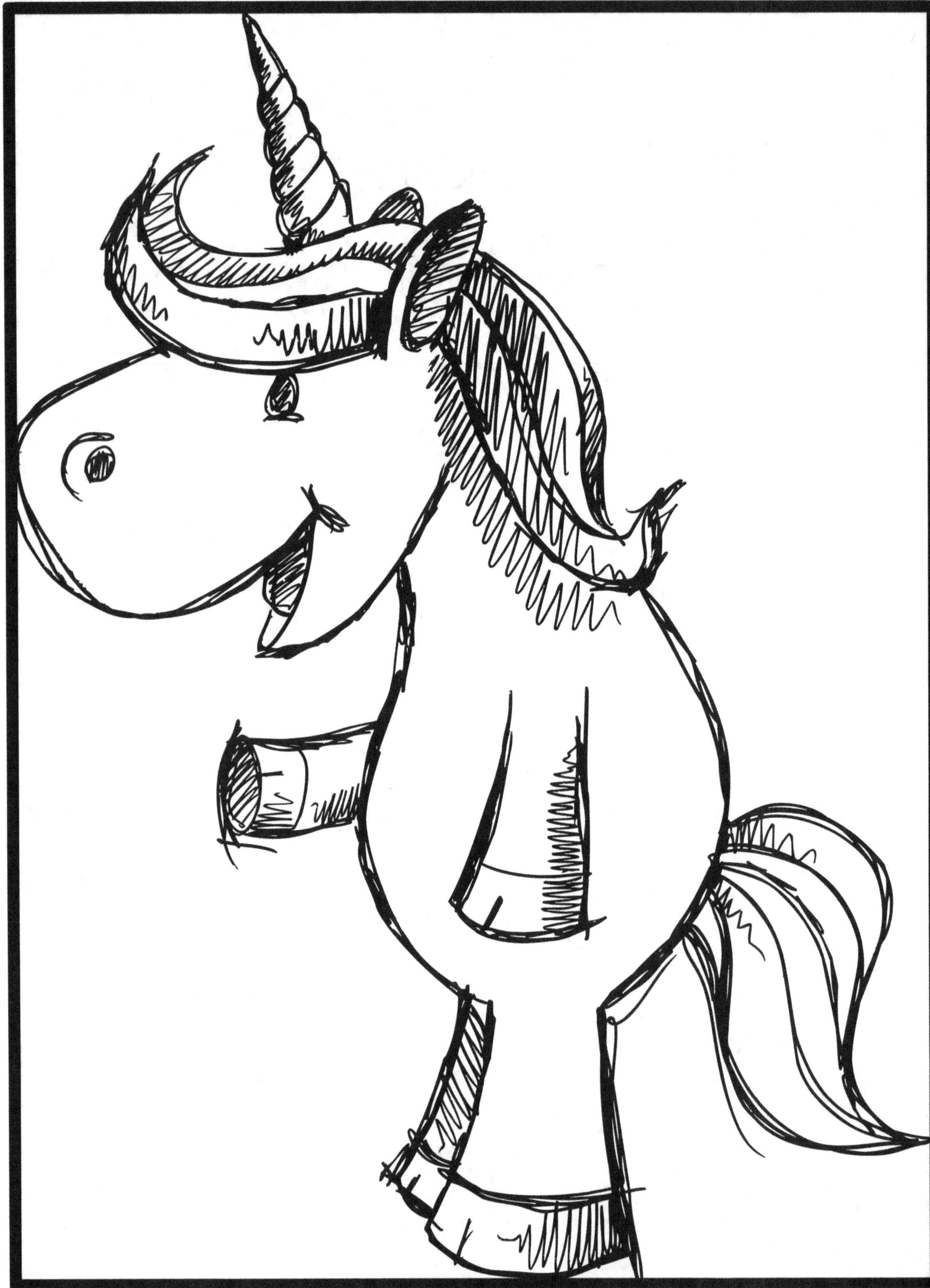

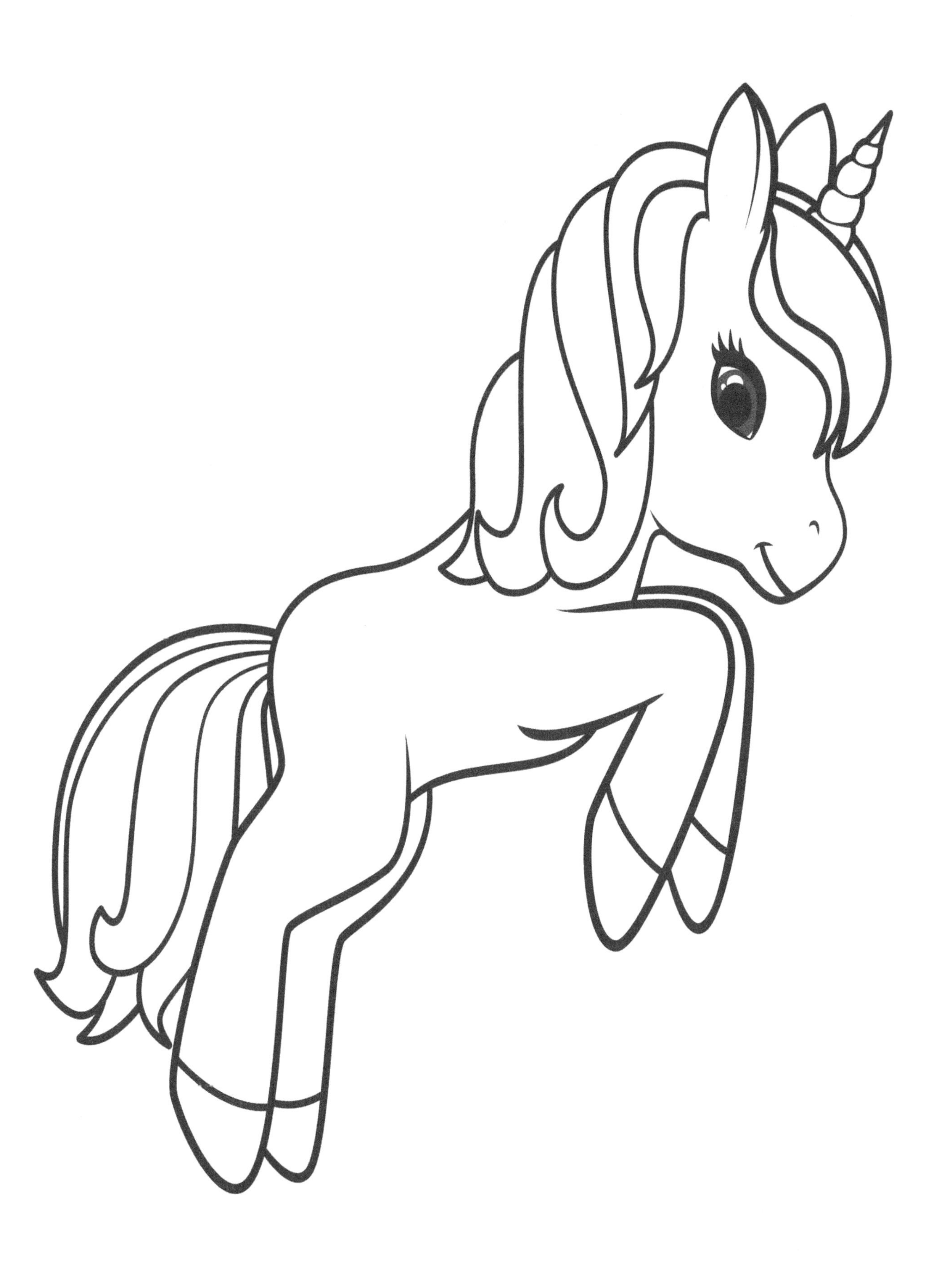

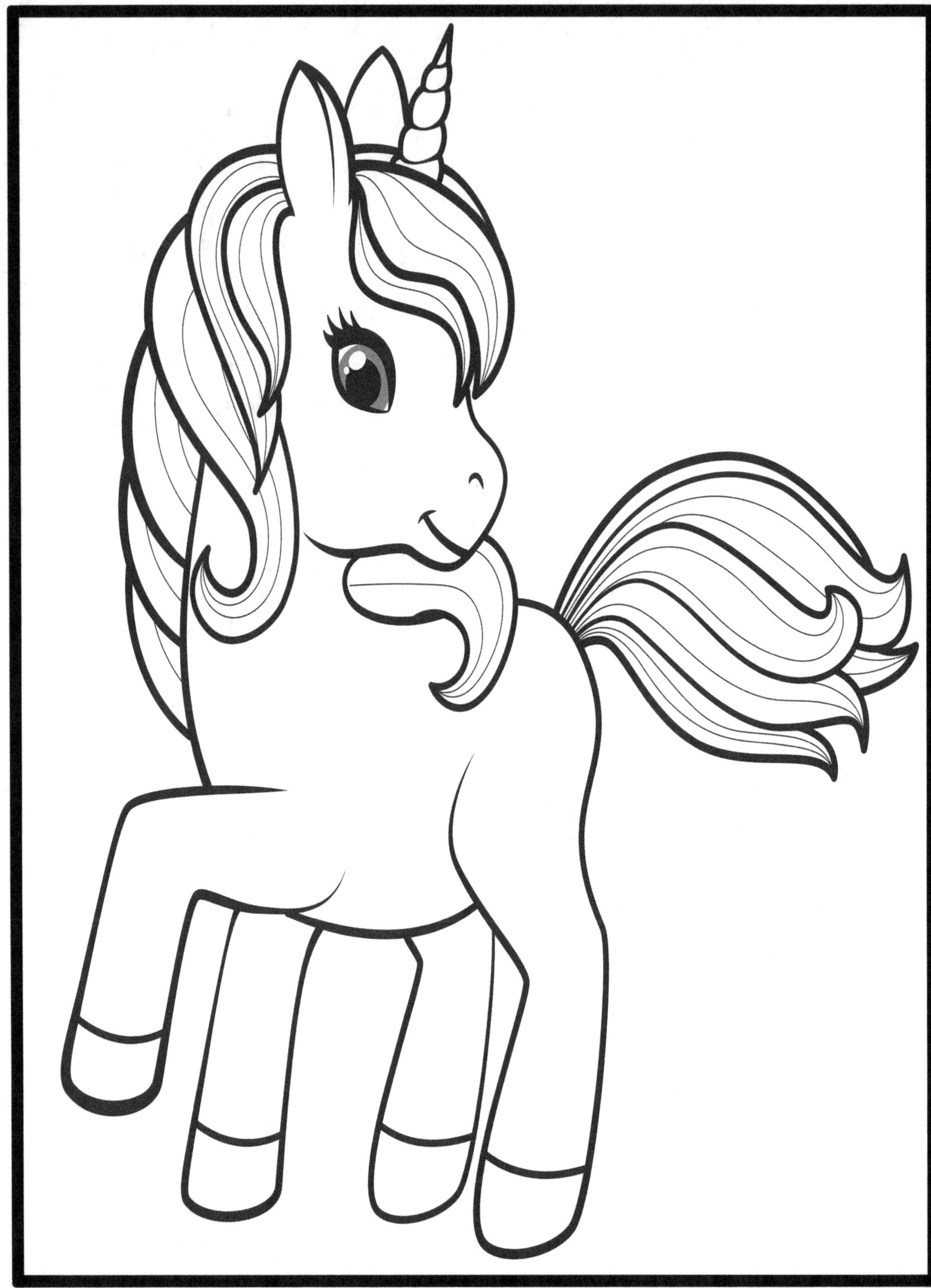

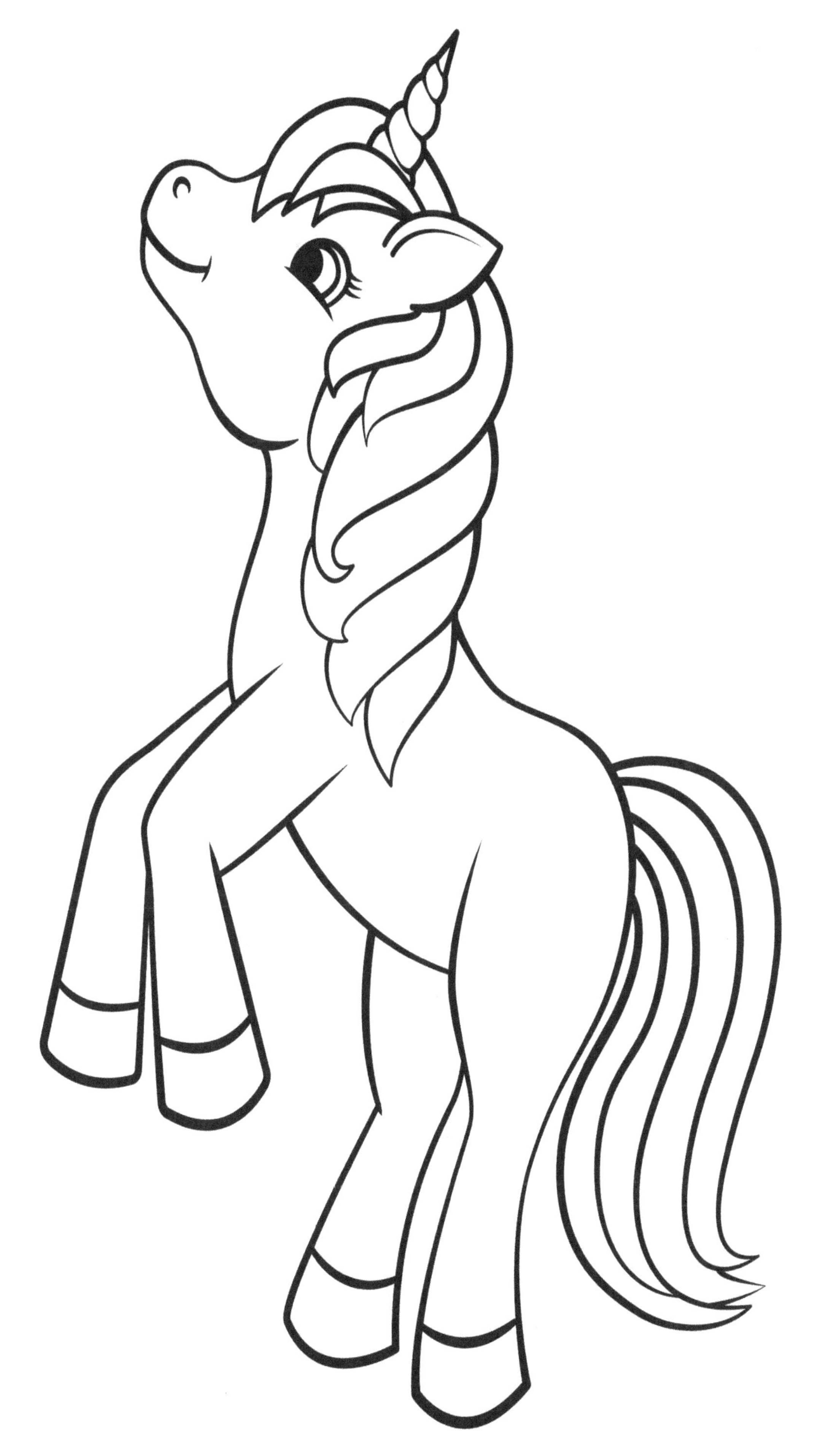

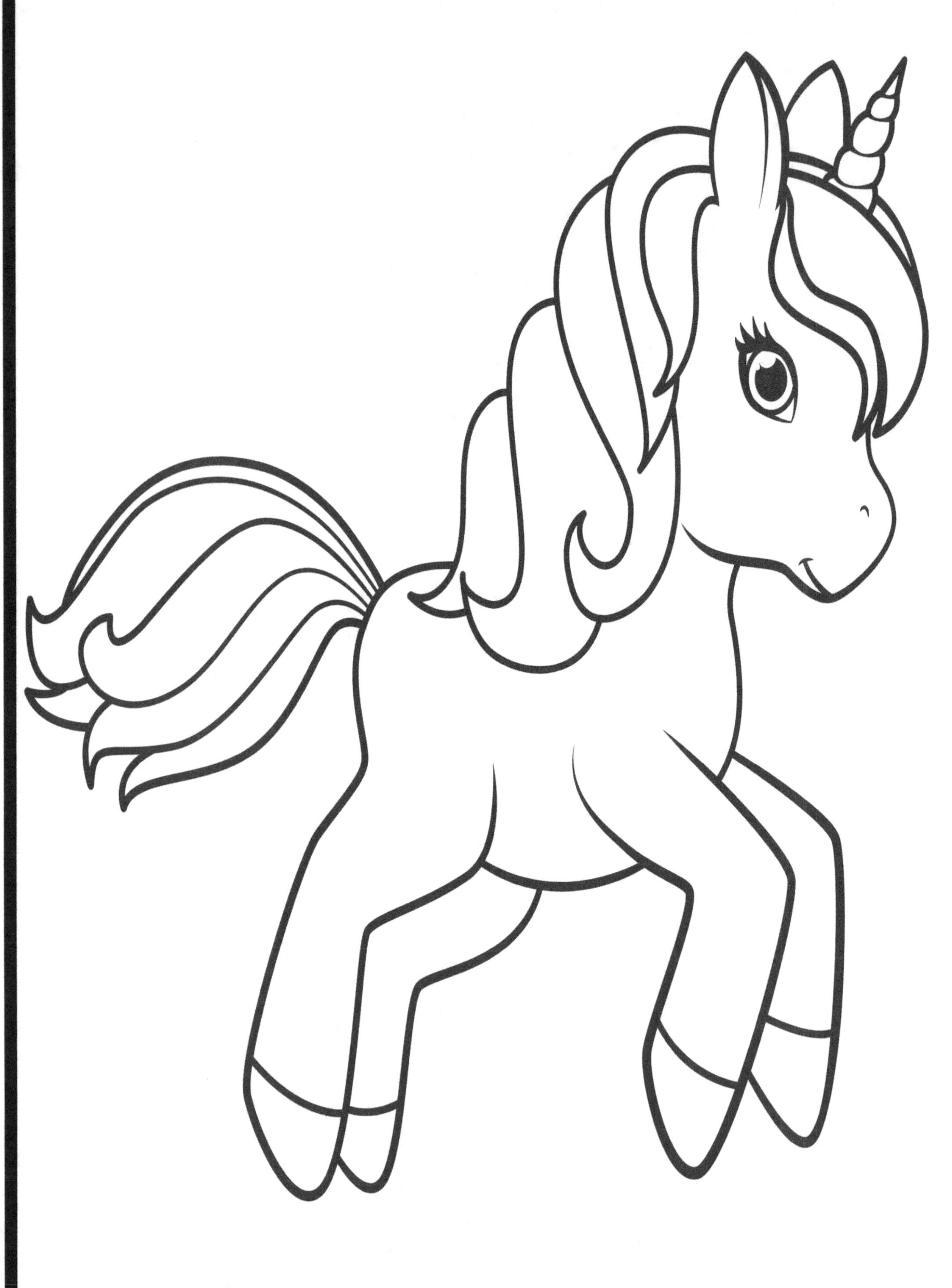

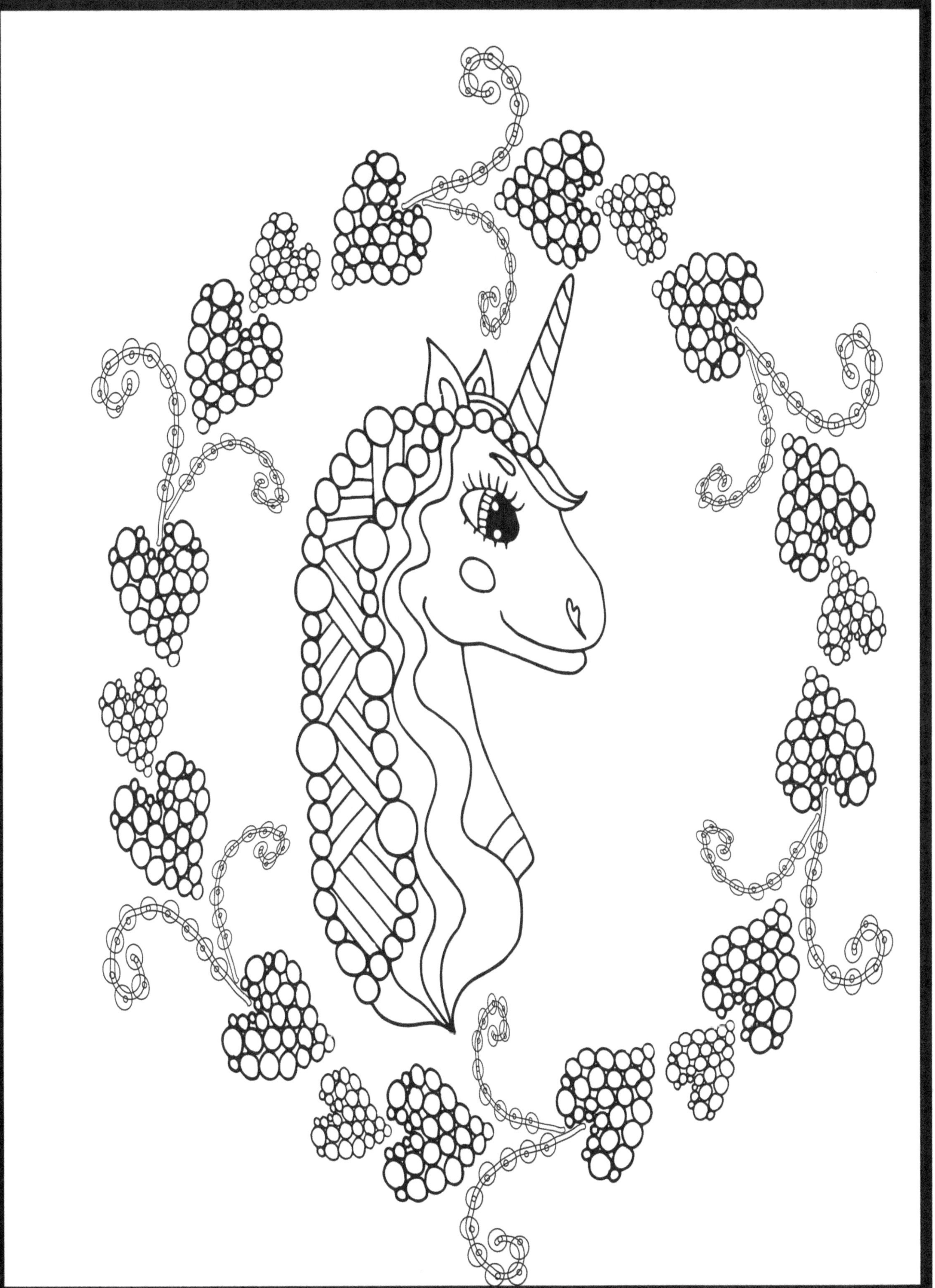

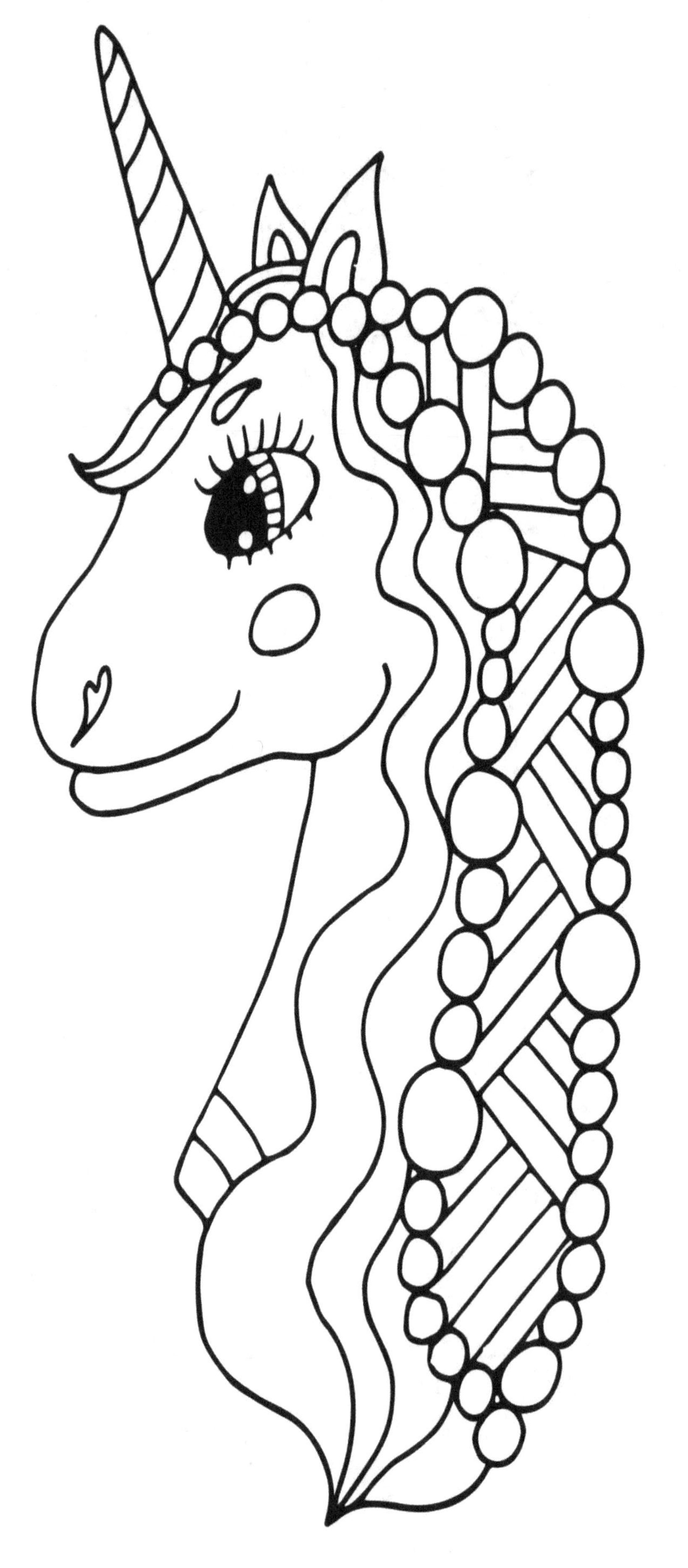

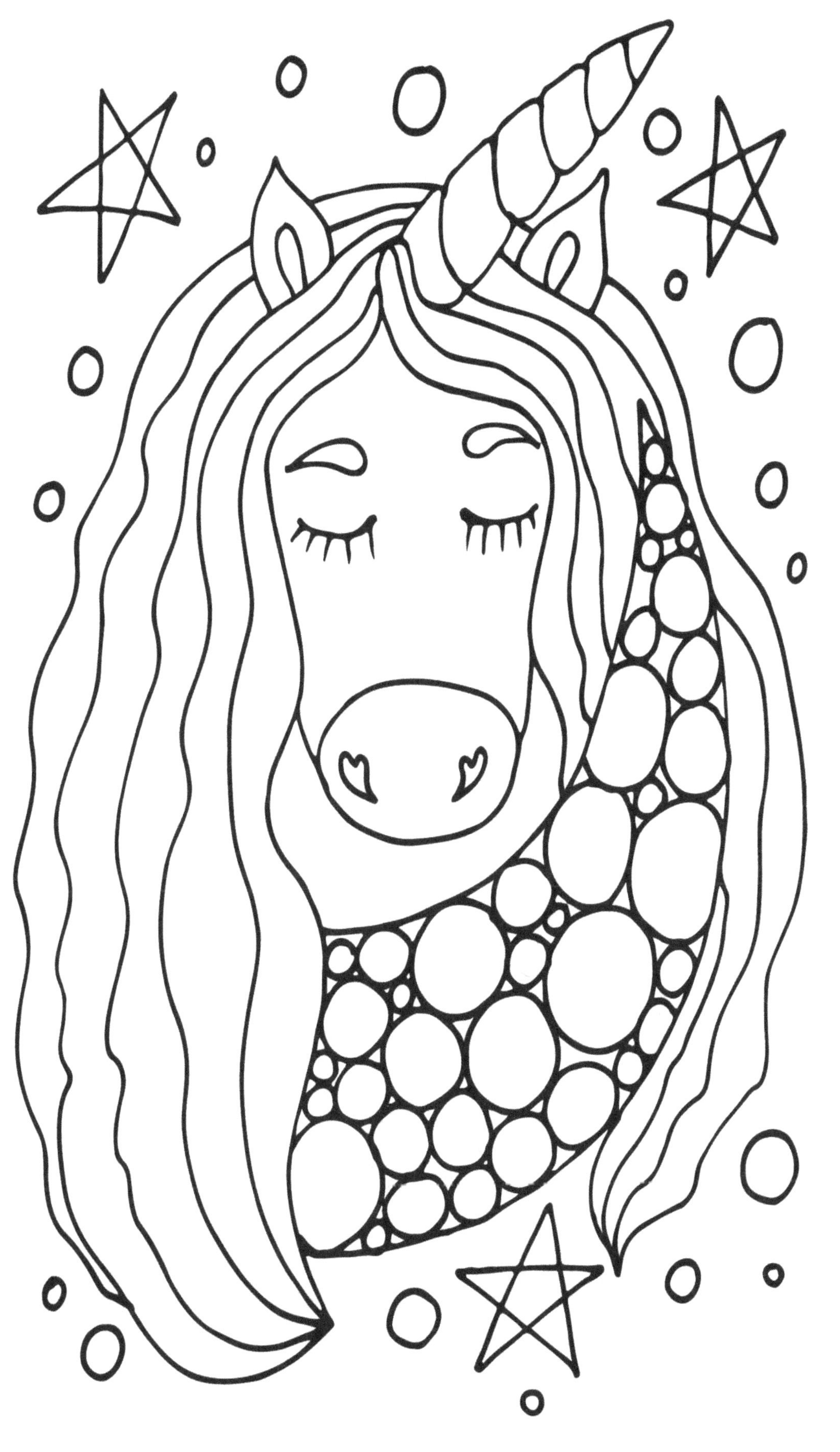

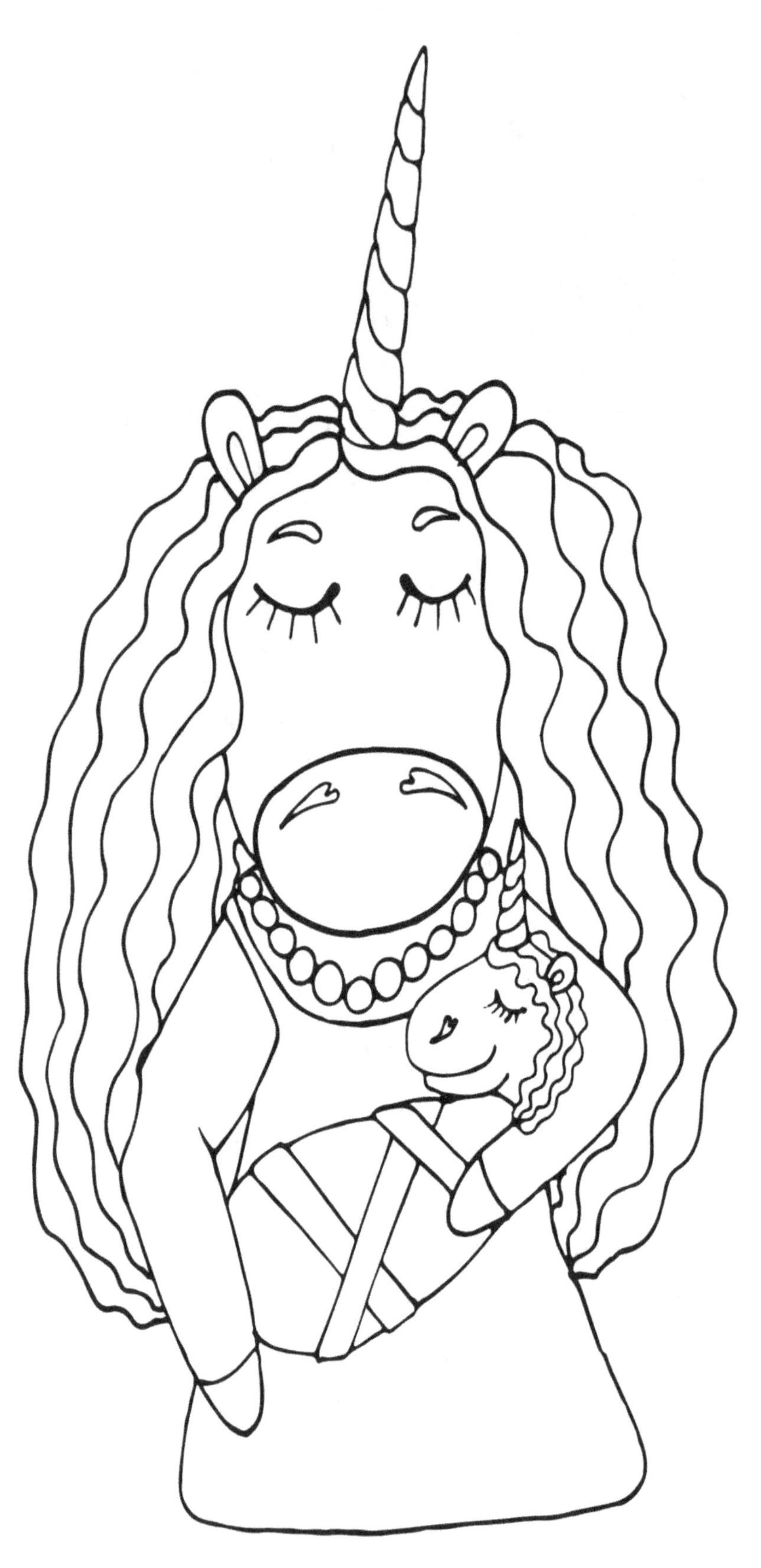

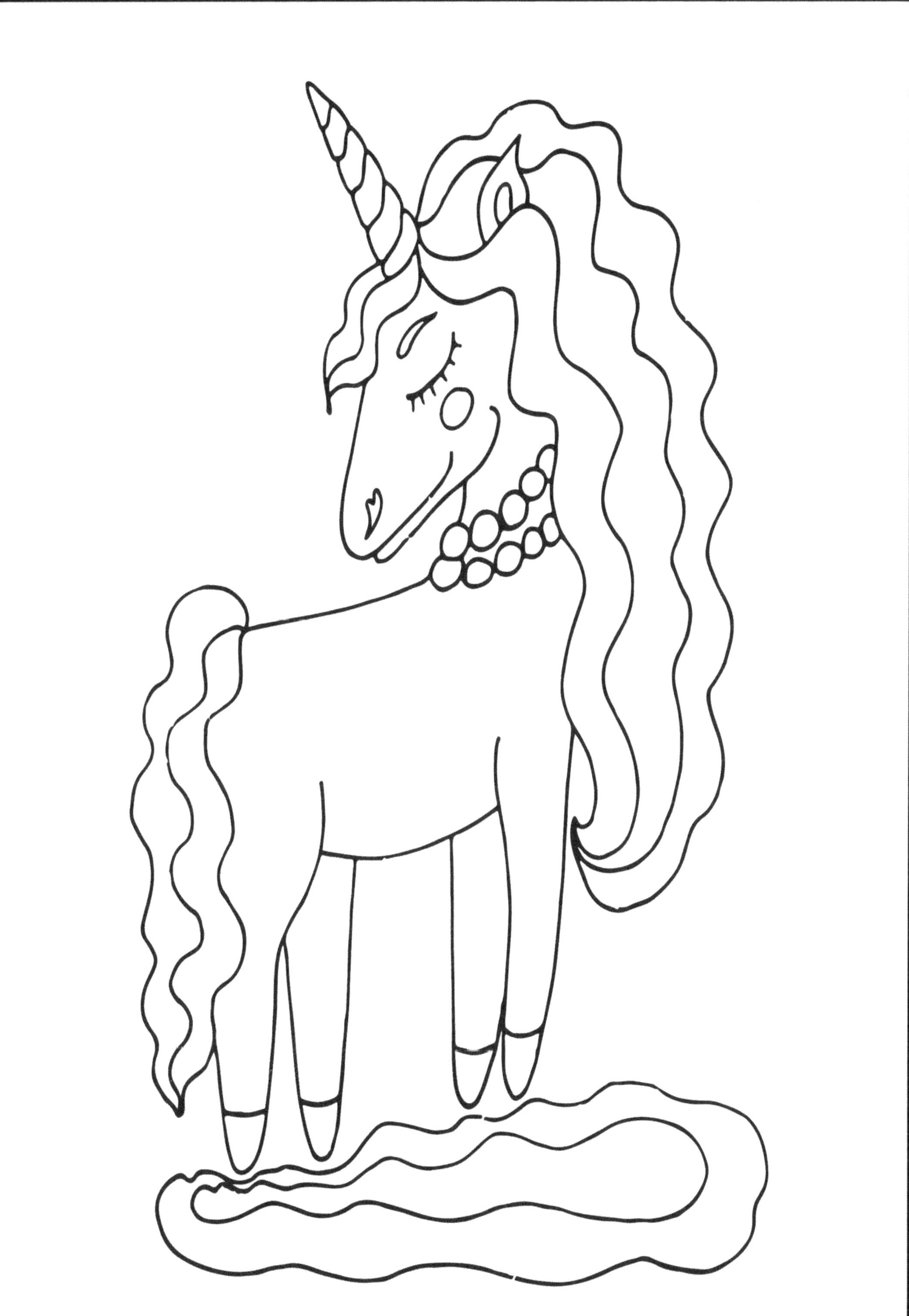

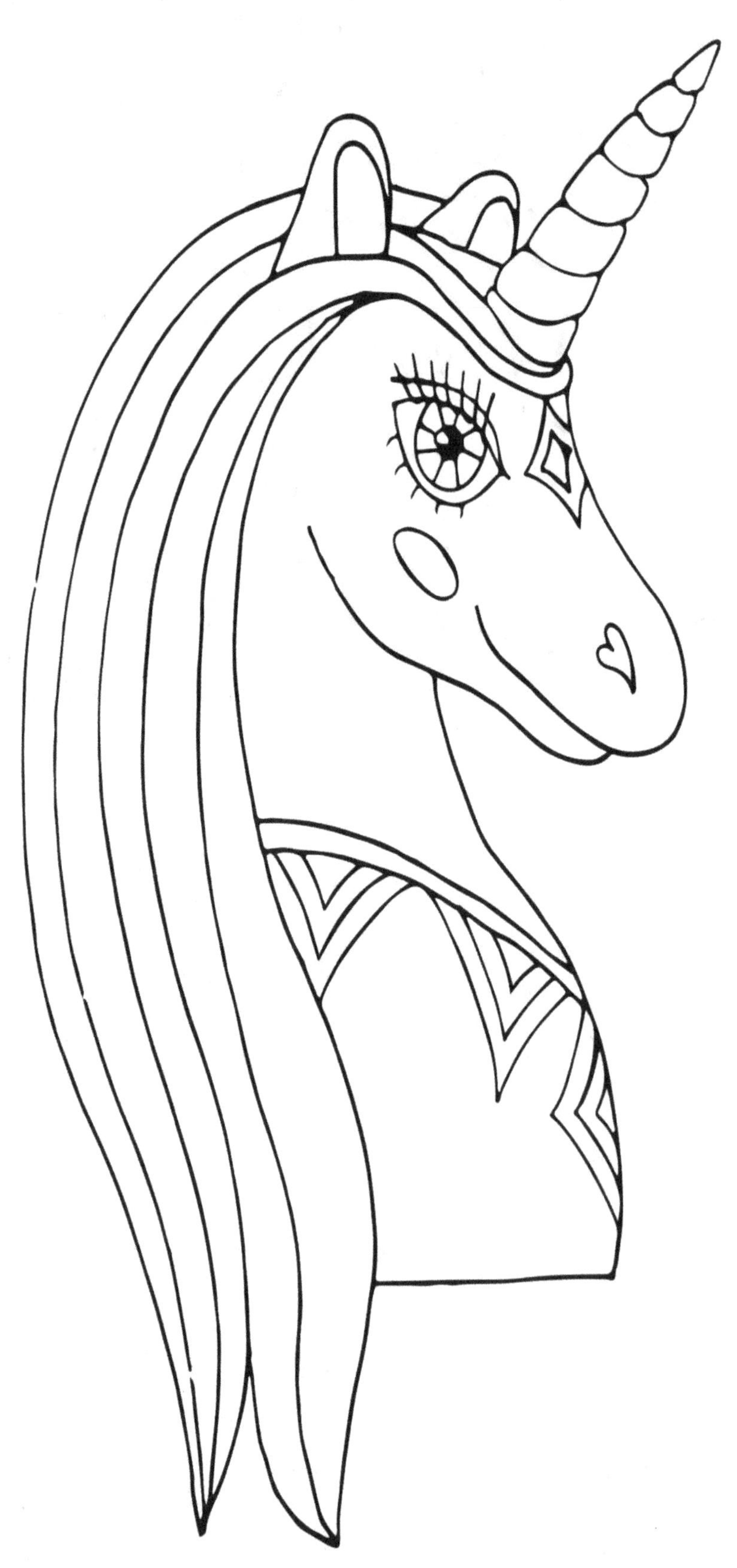

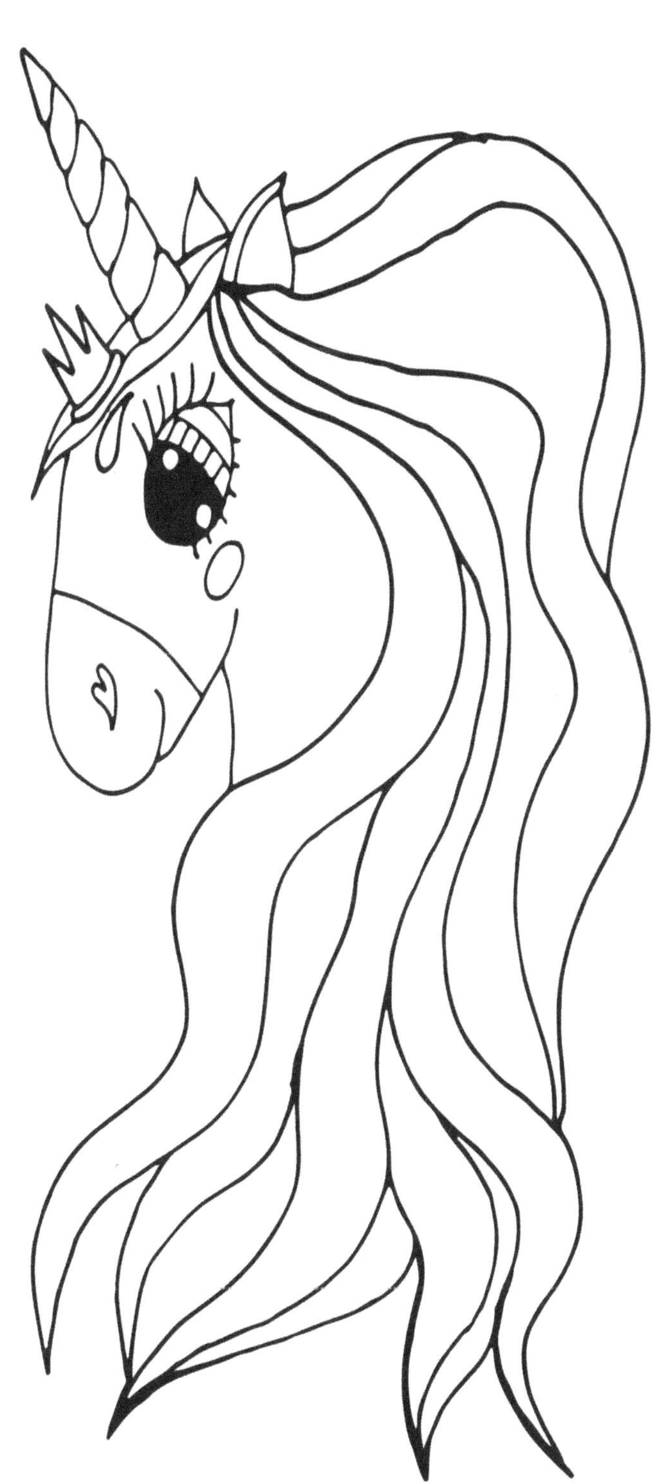

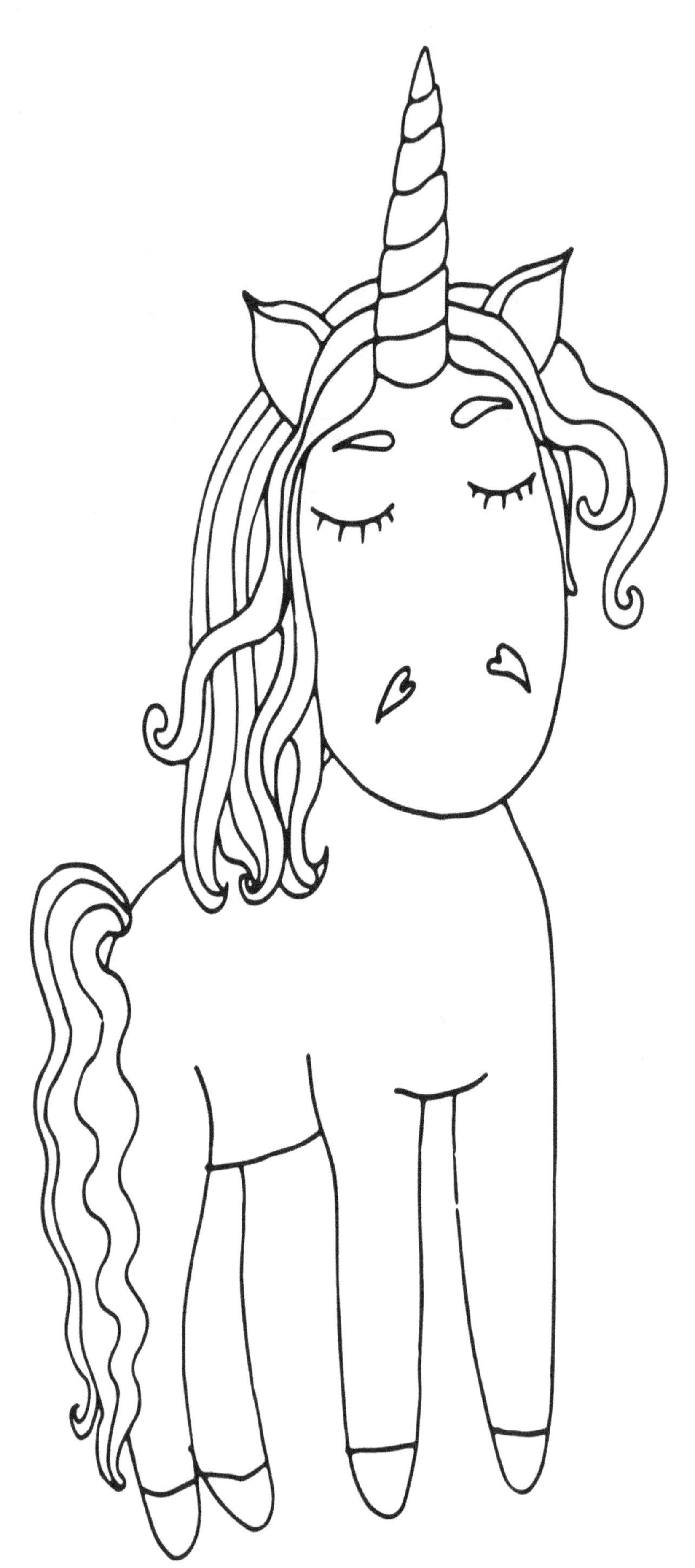

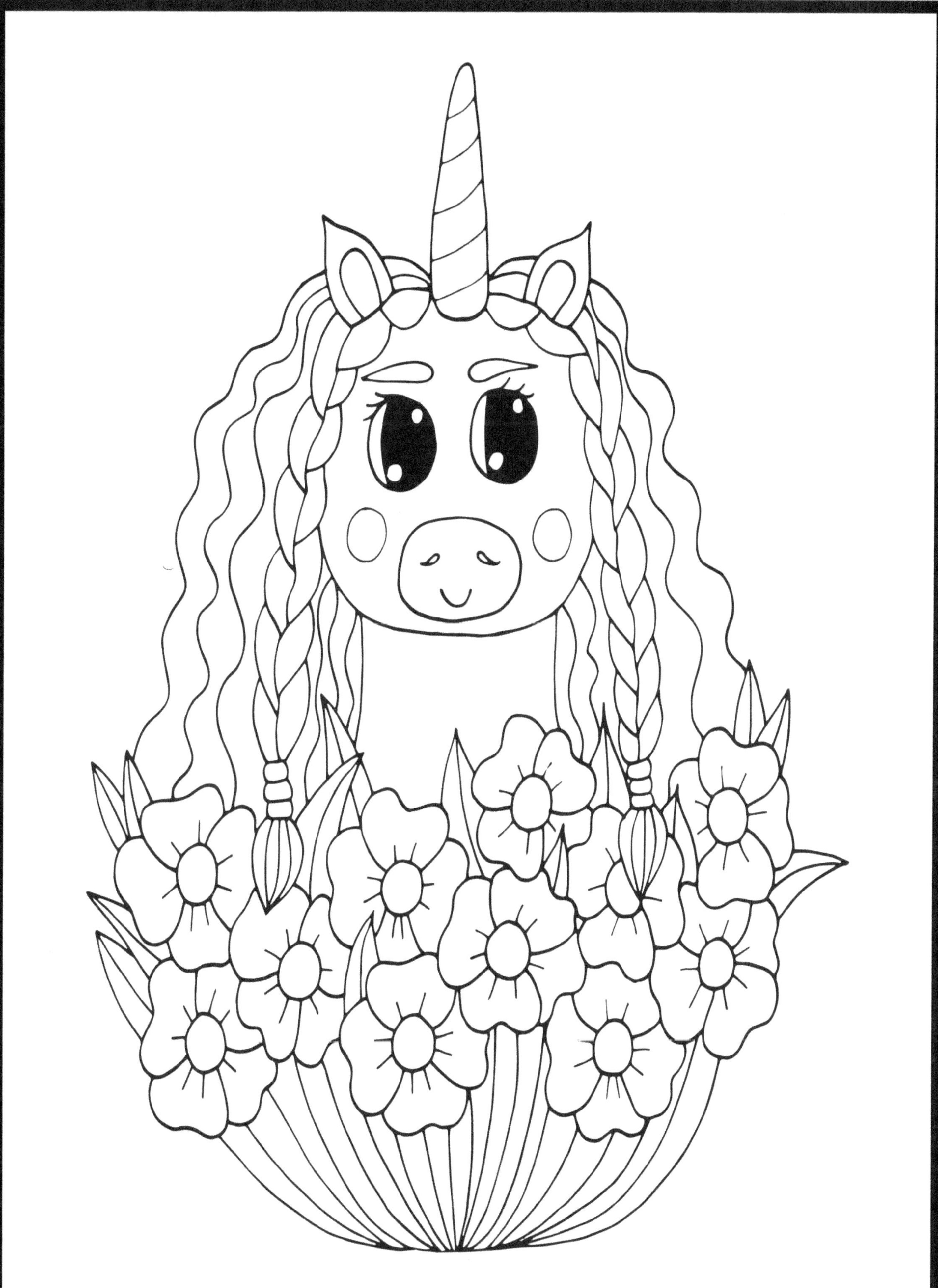

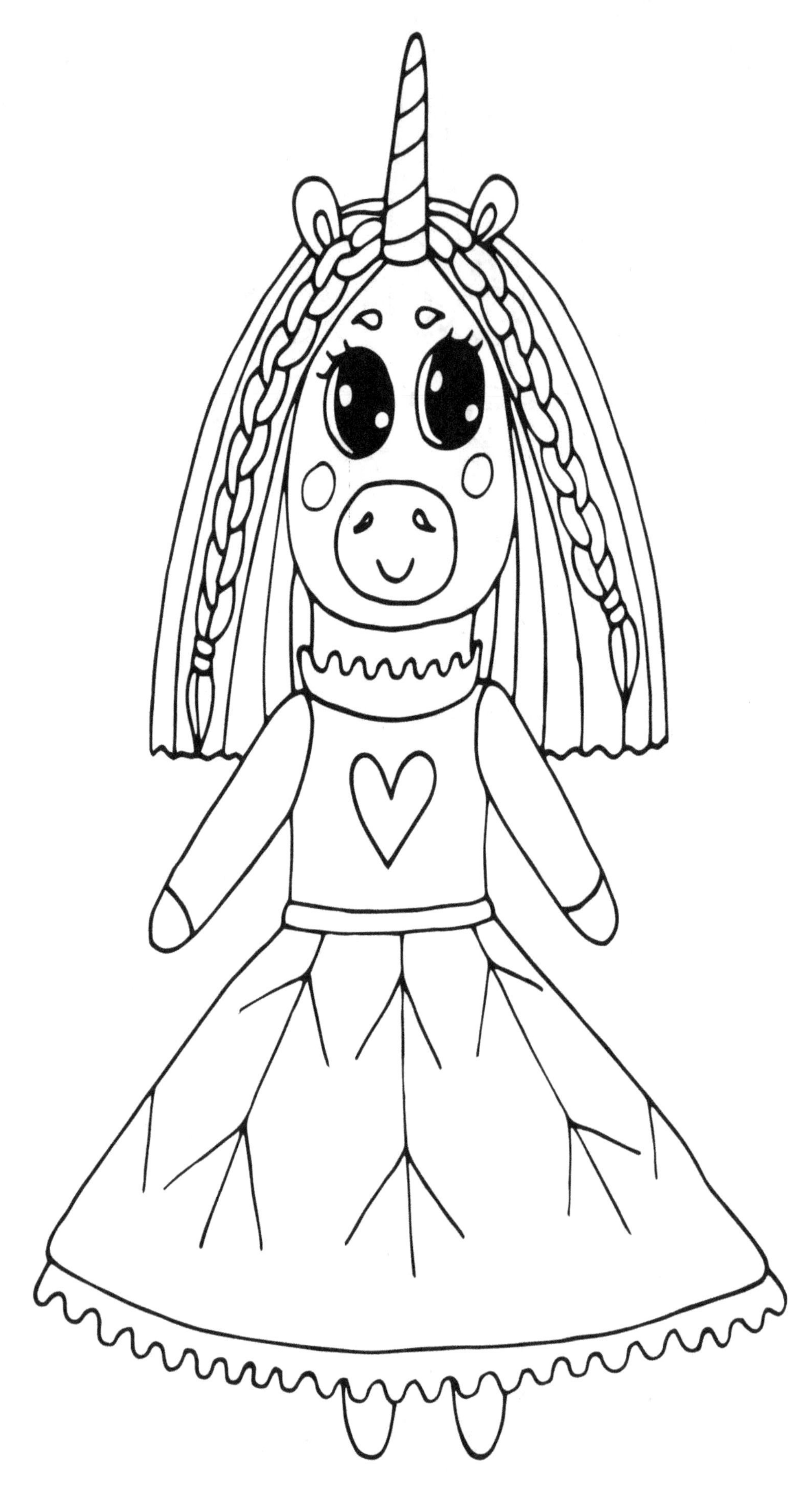

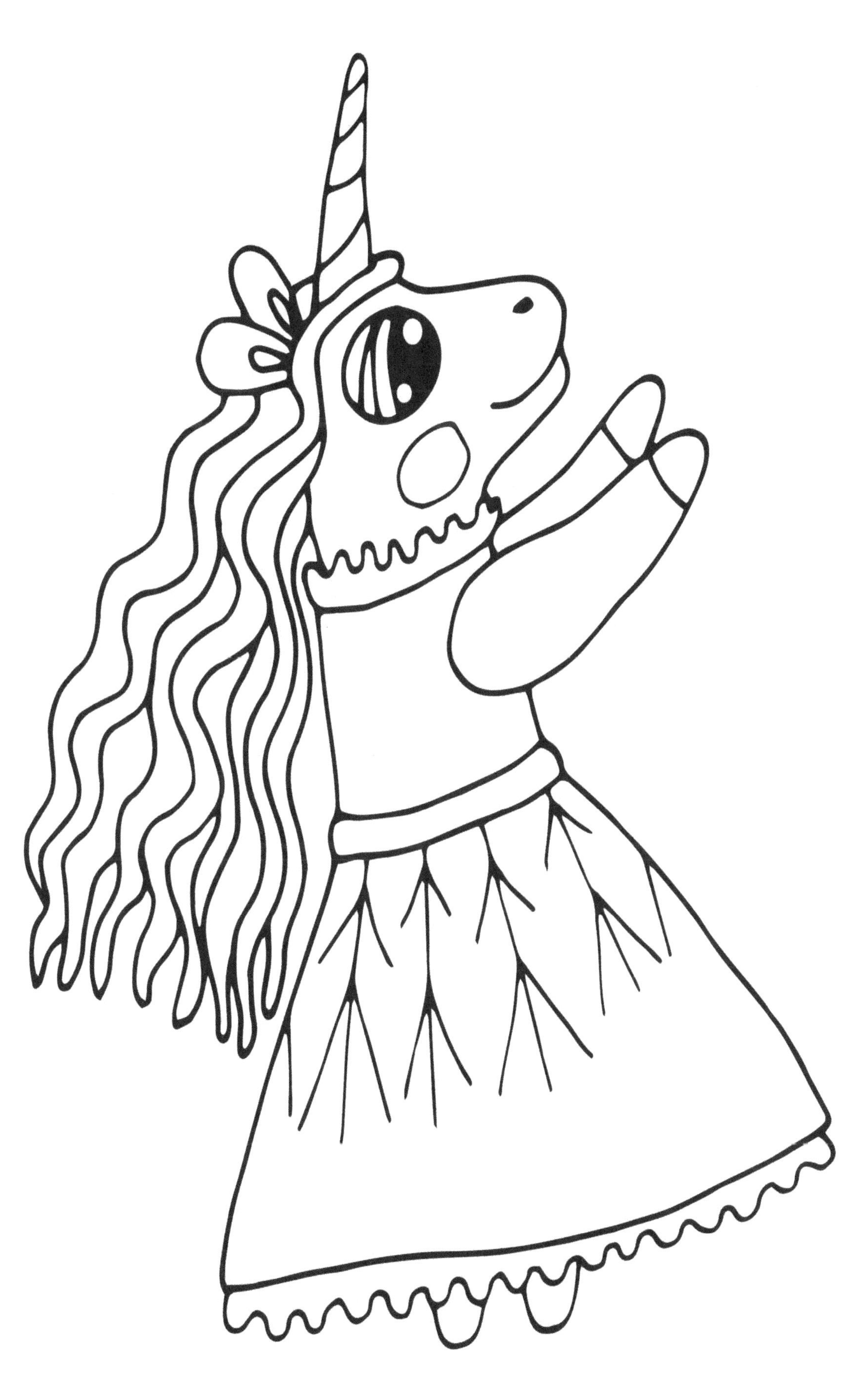

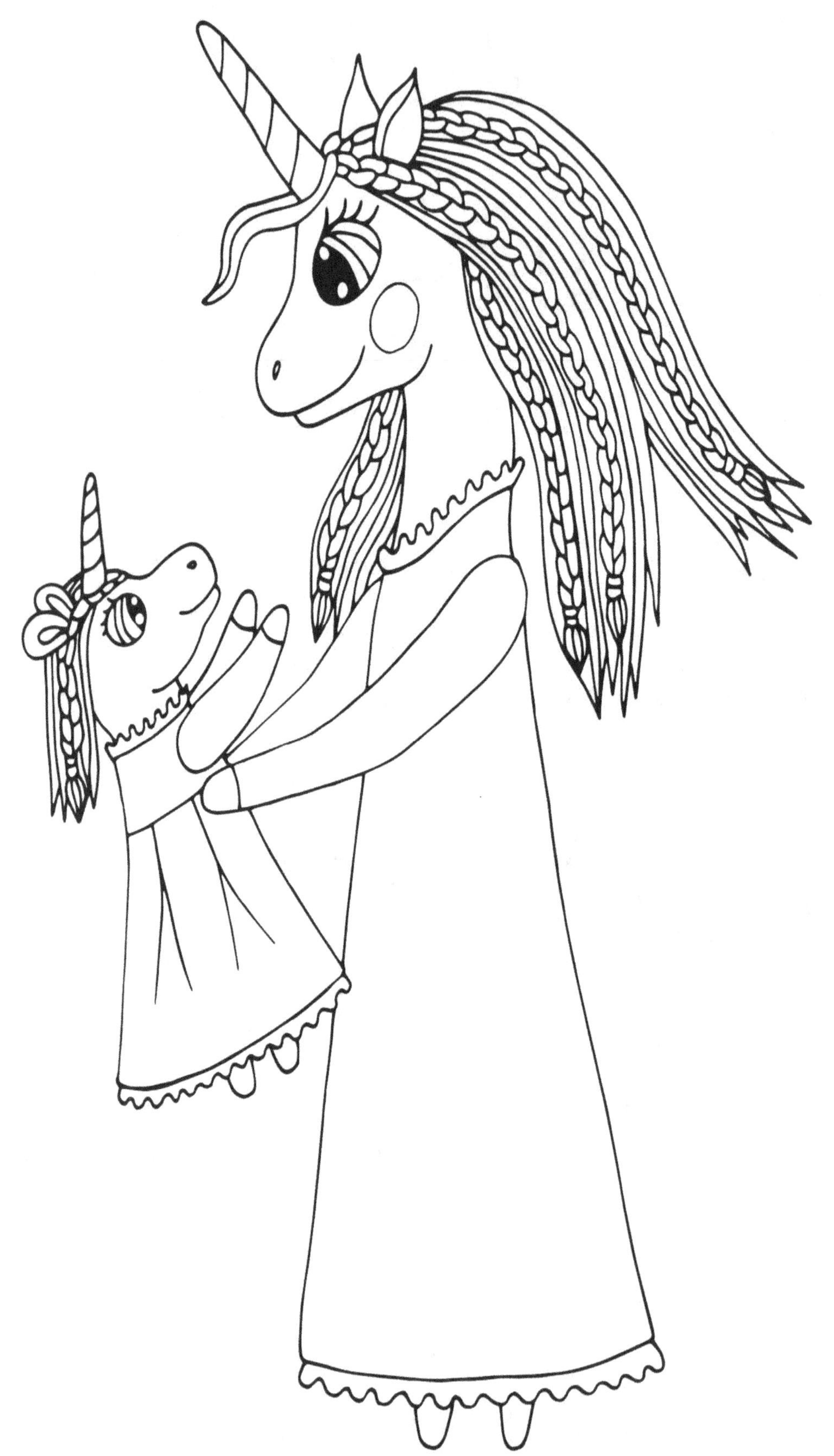

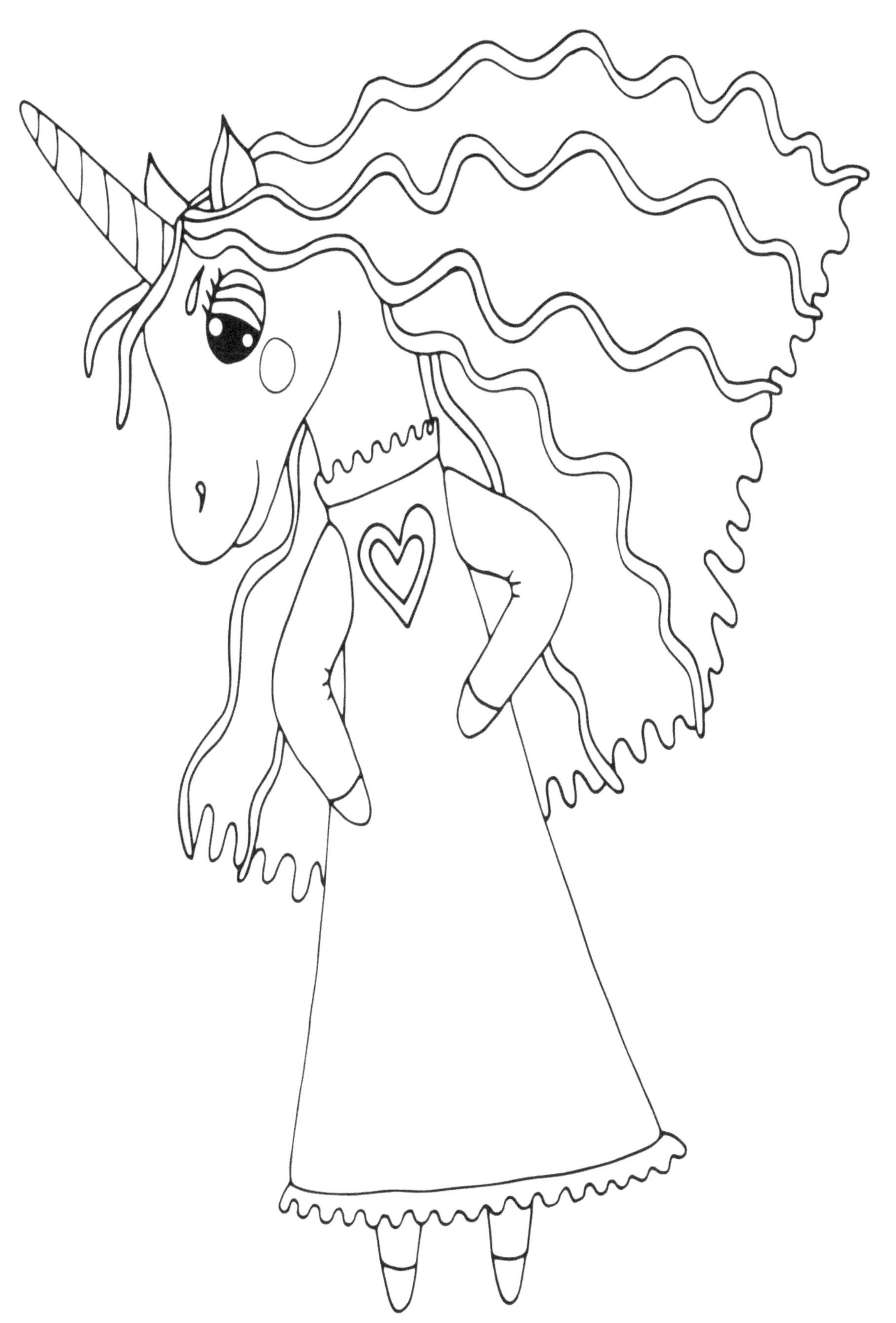

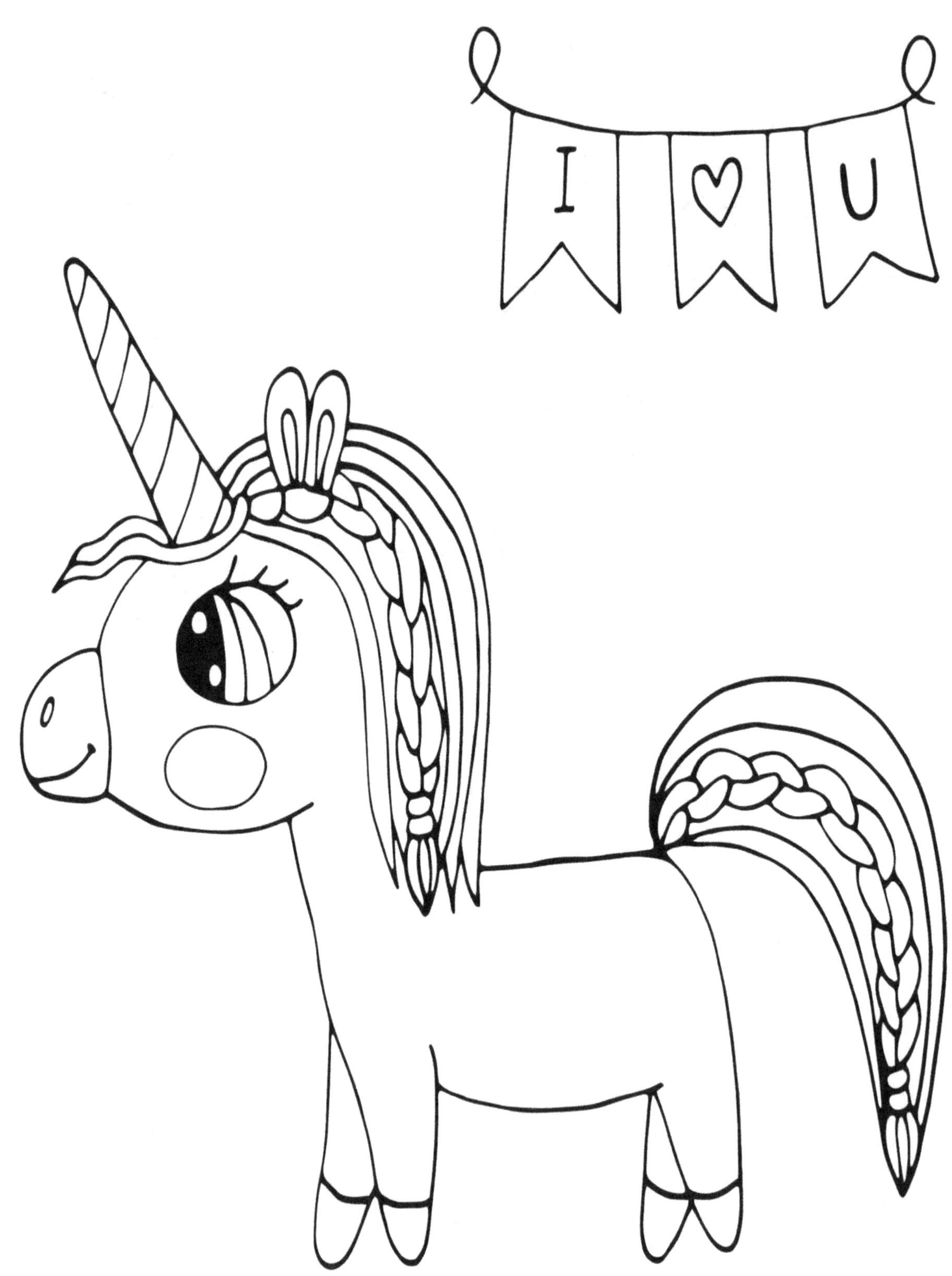

I ♥ U

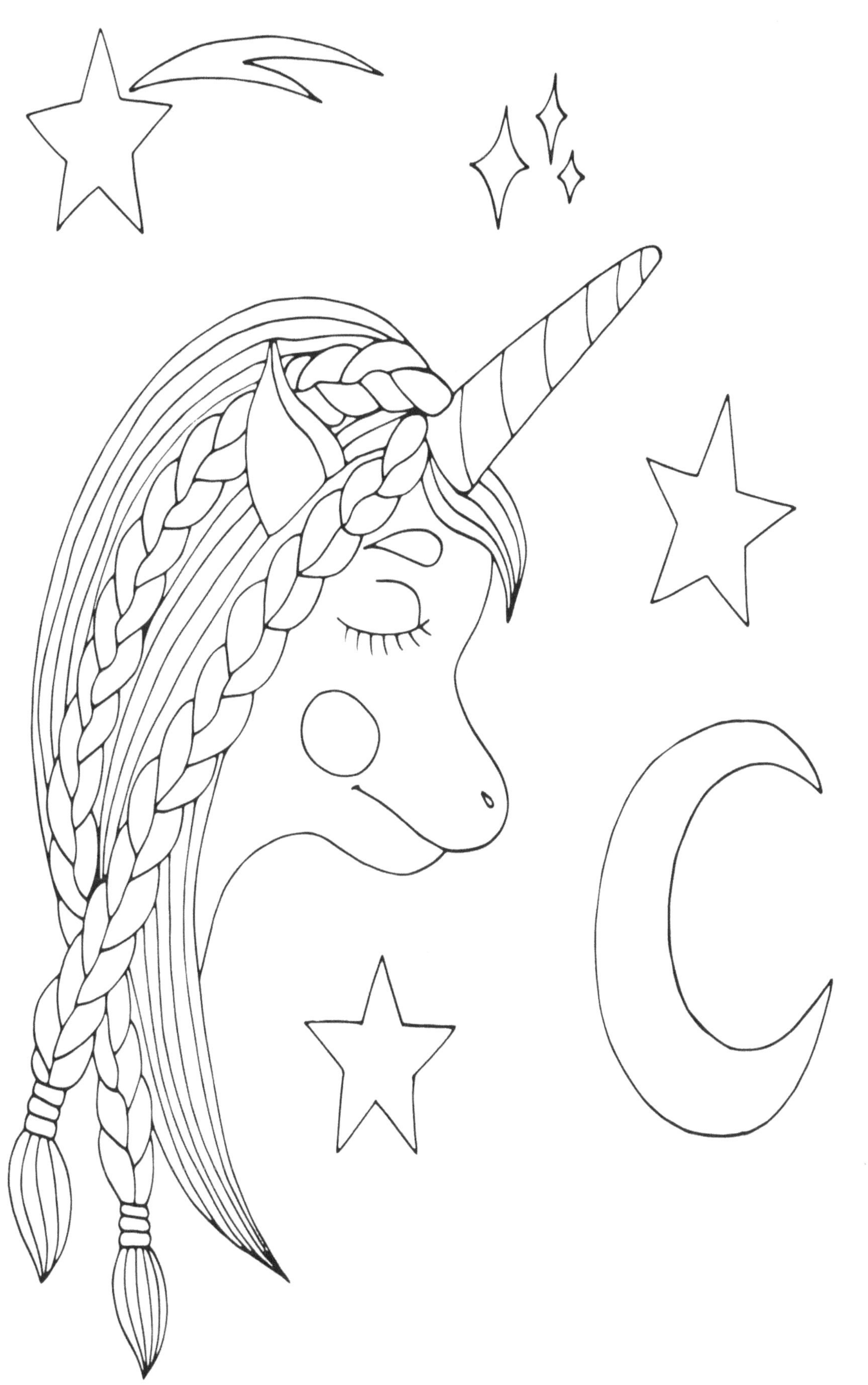

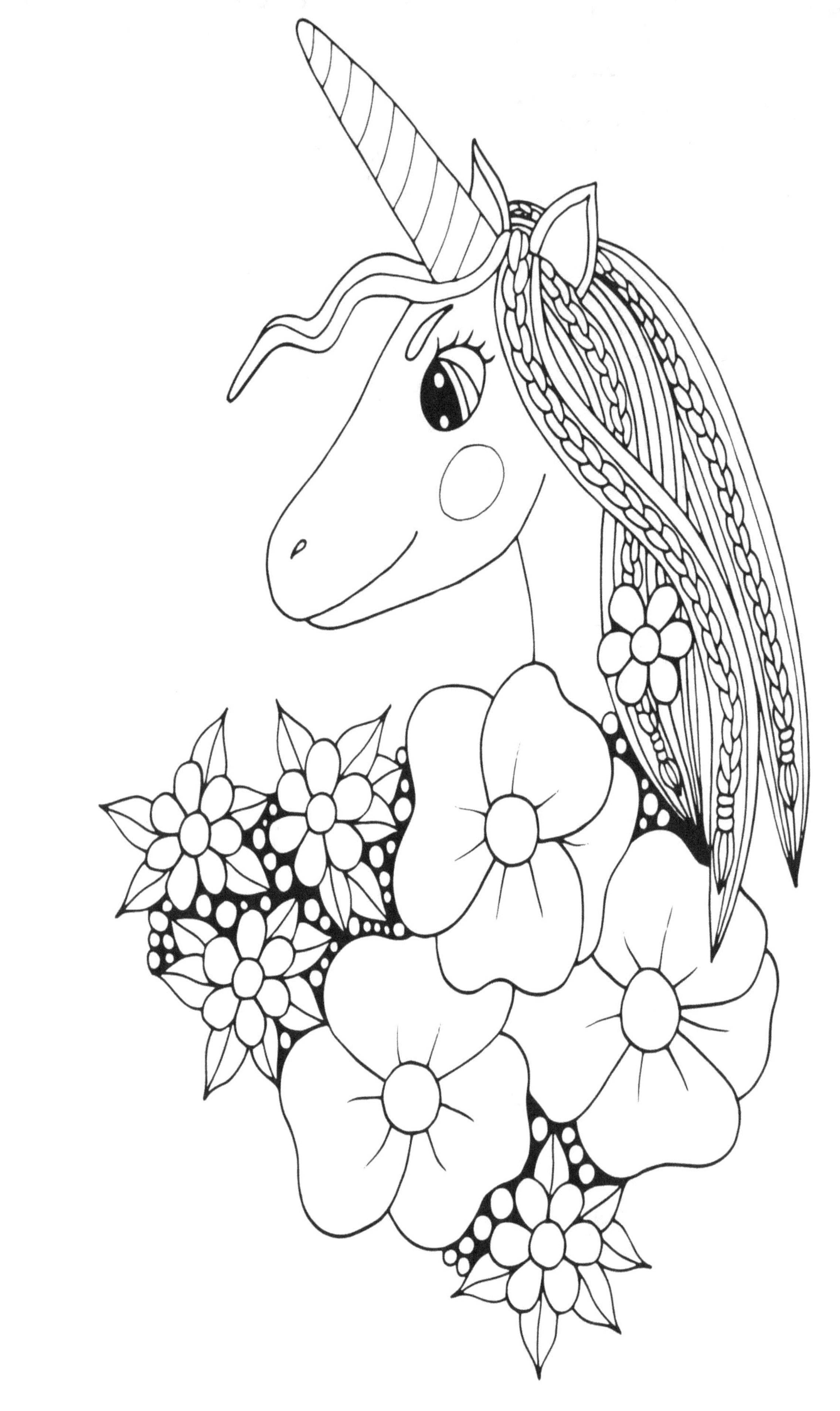

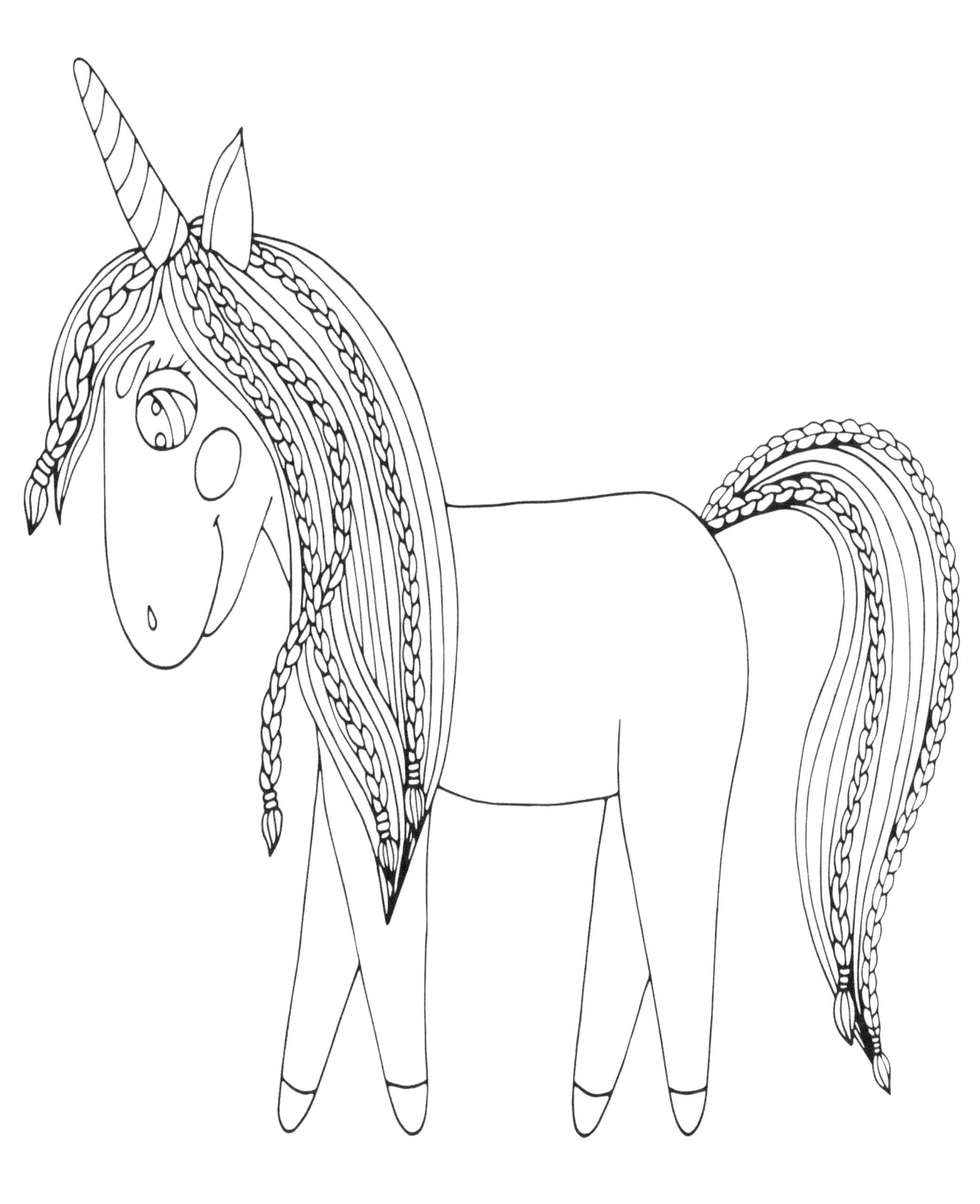

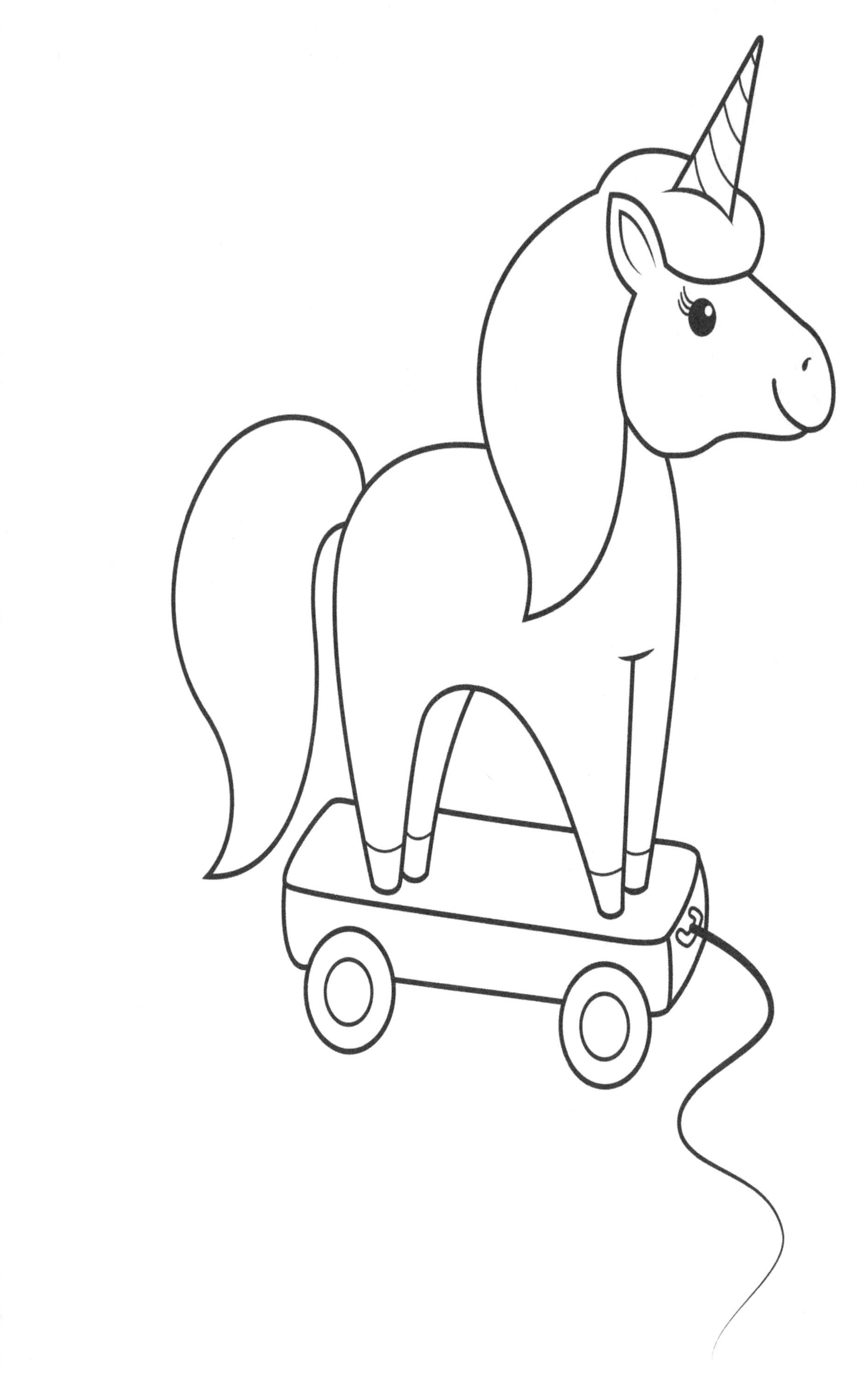

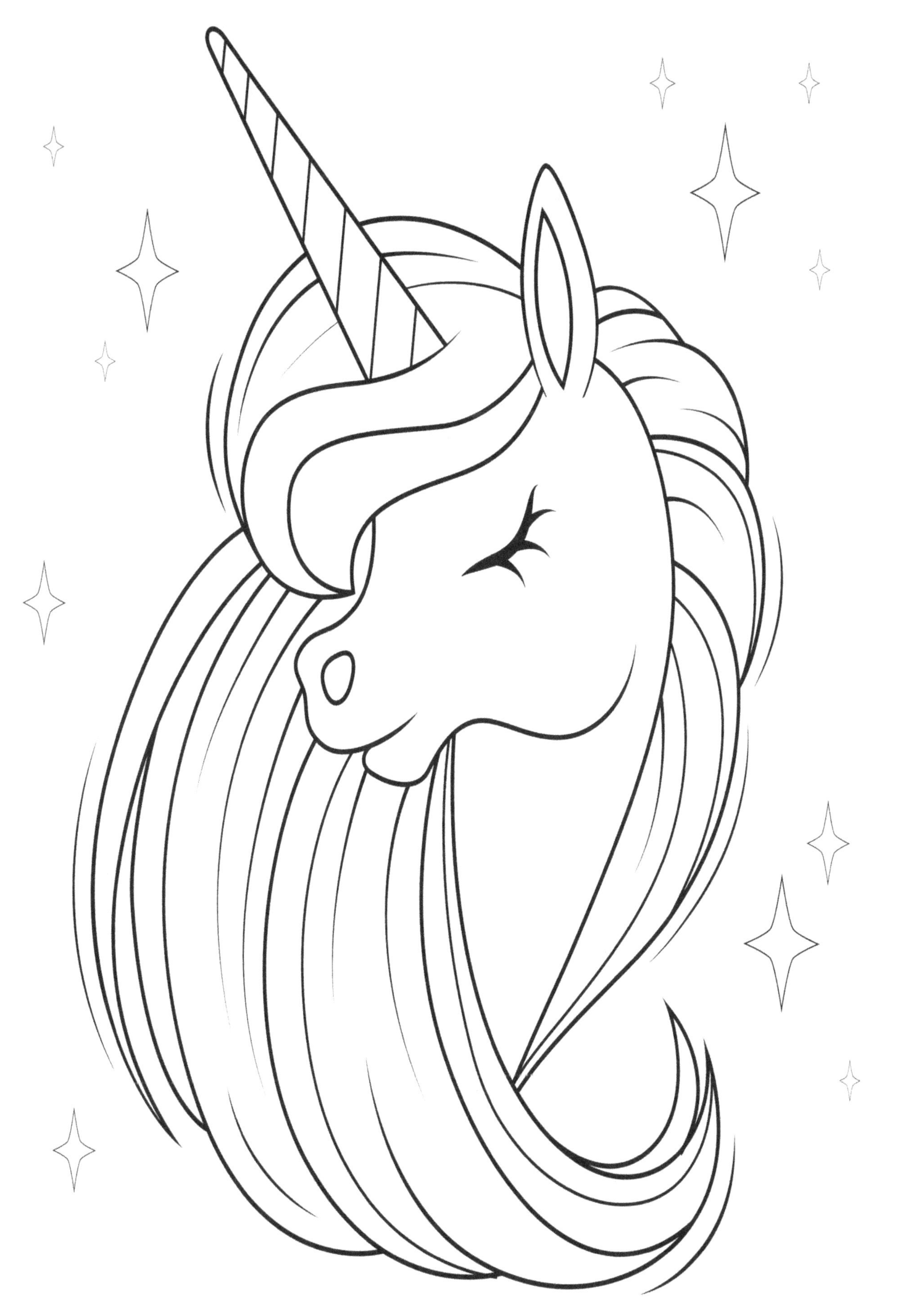

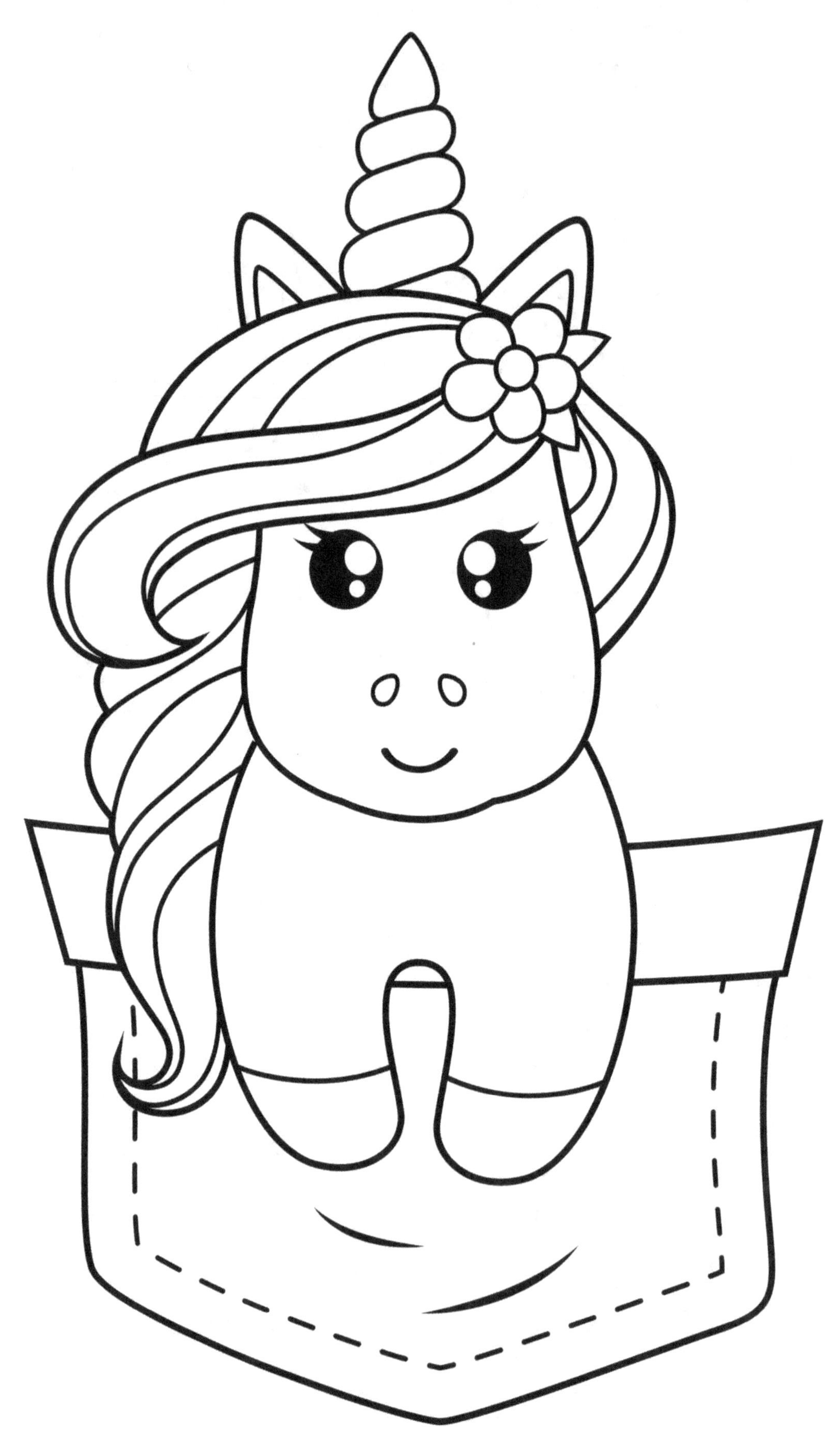

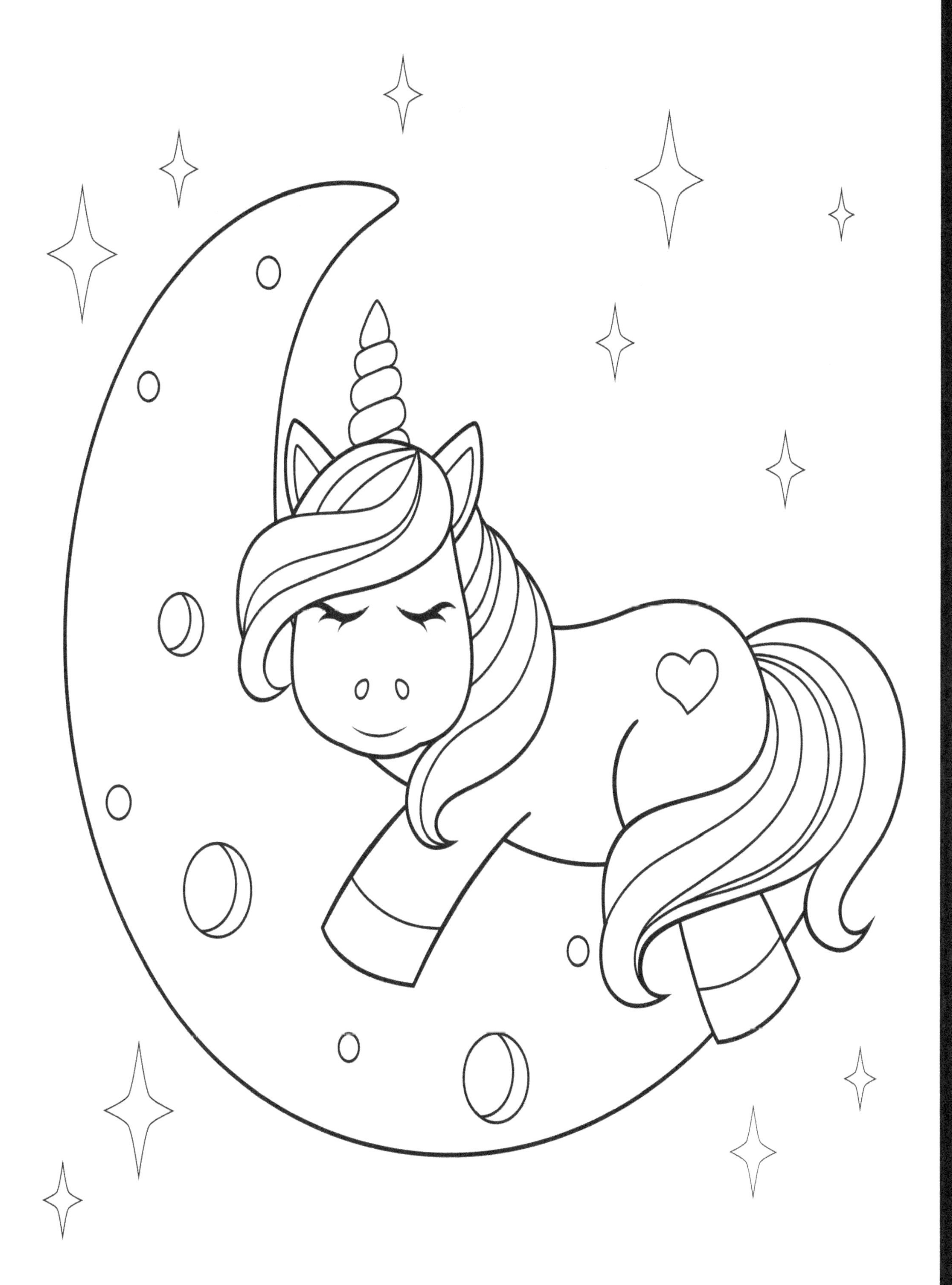

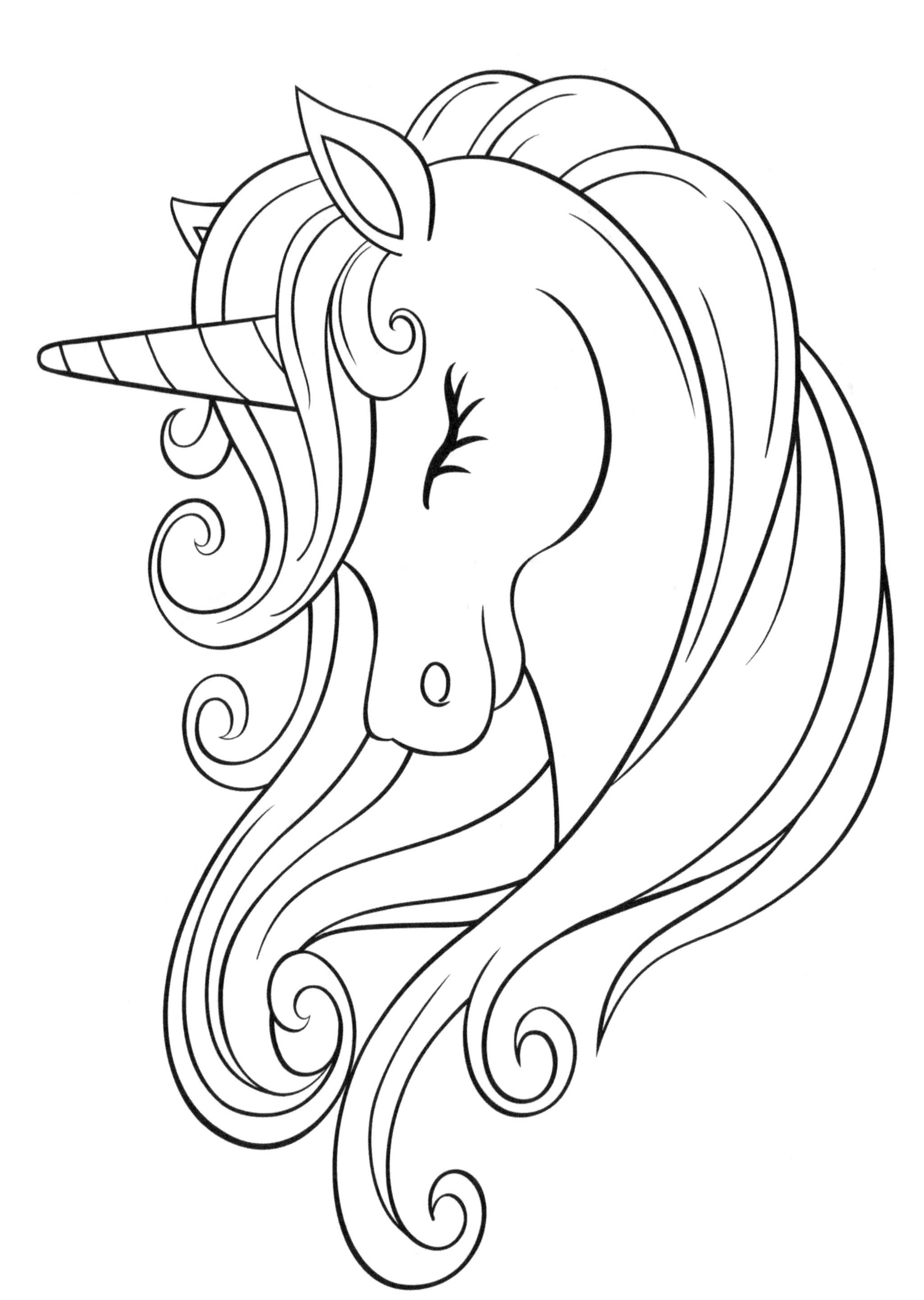

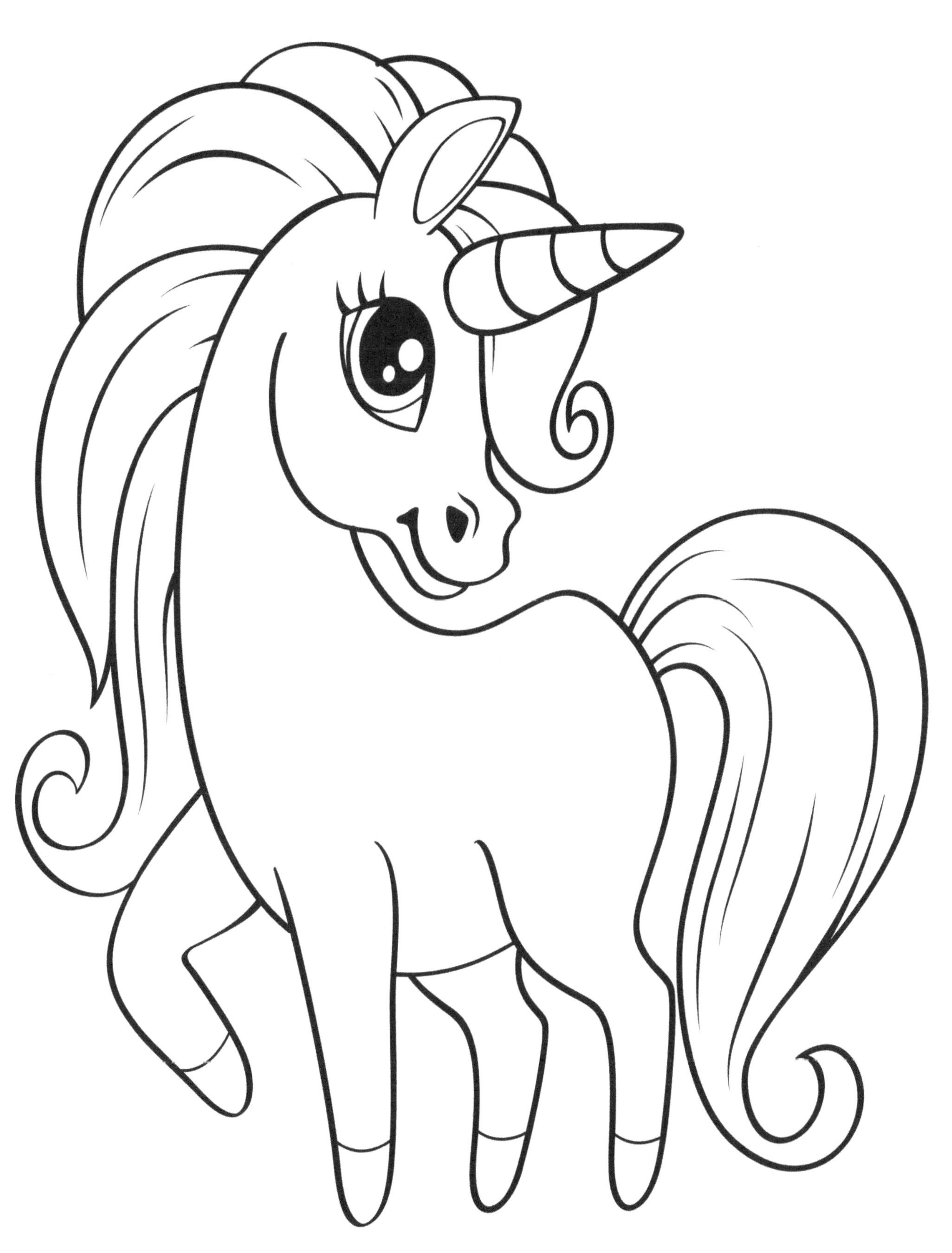

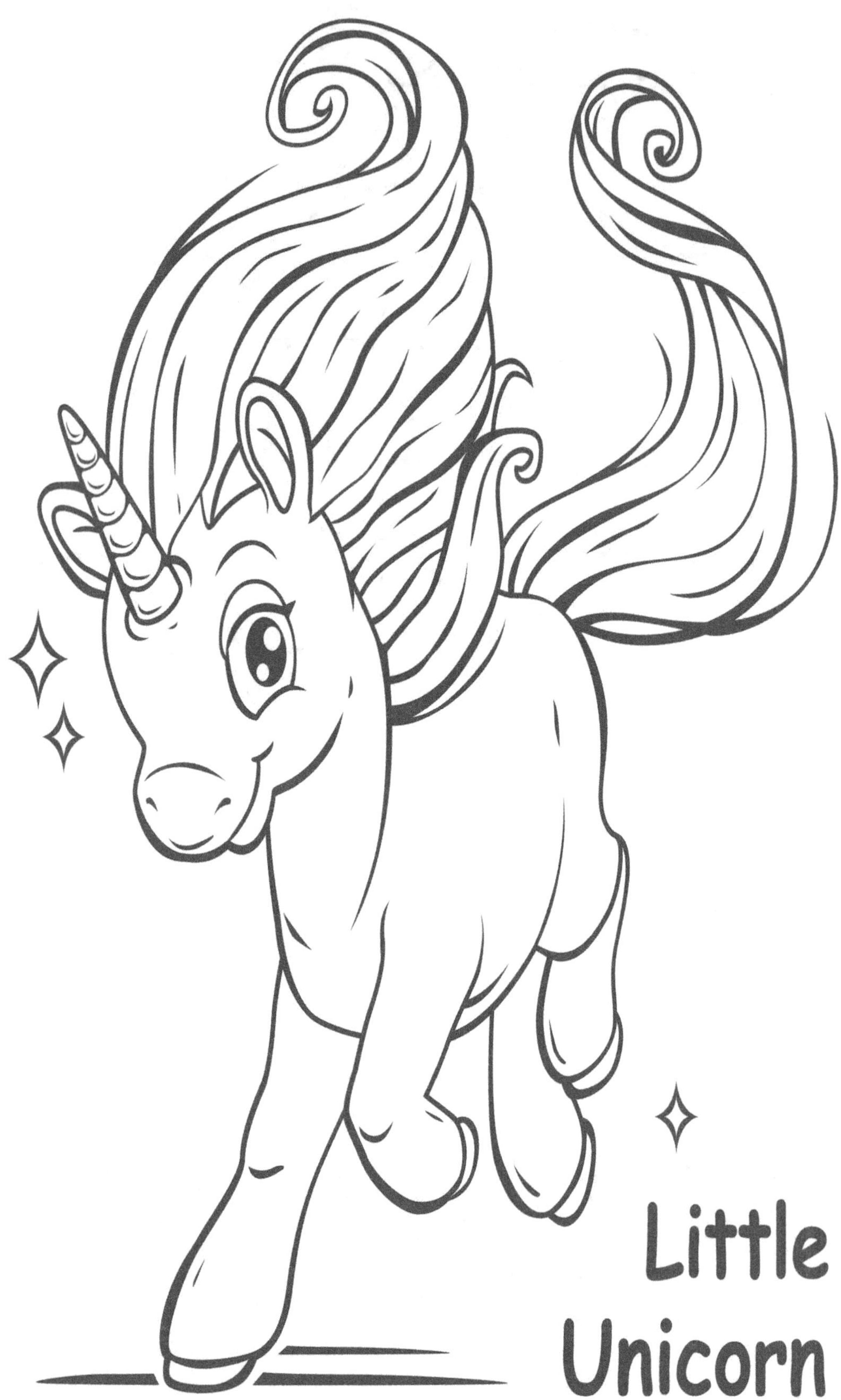

Little
Unicorn

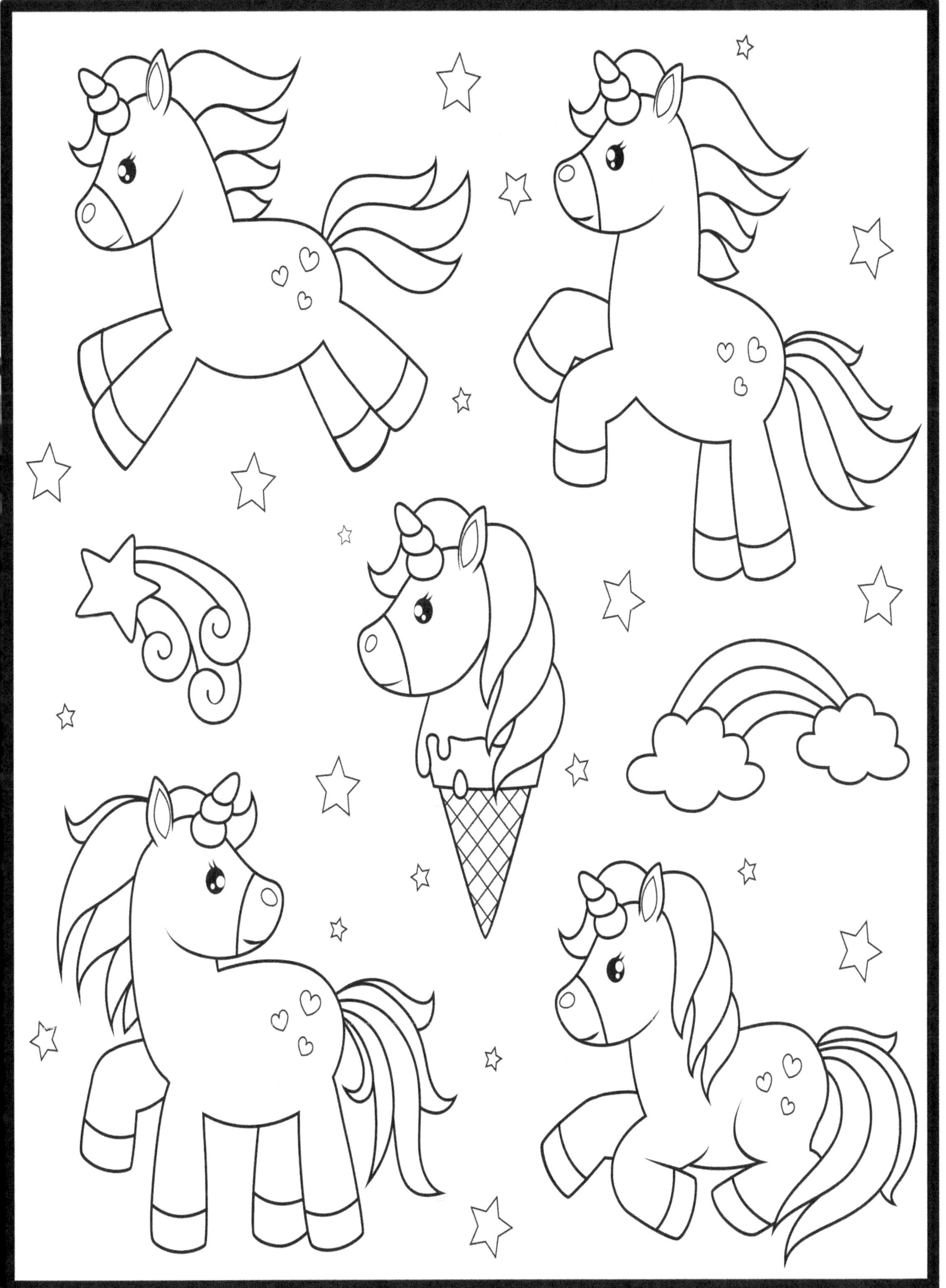

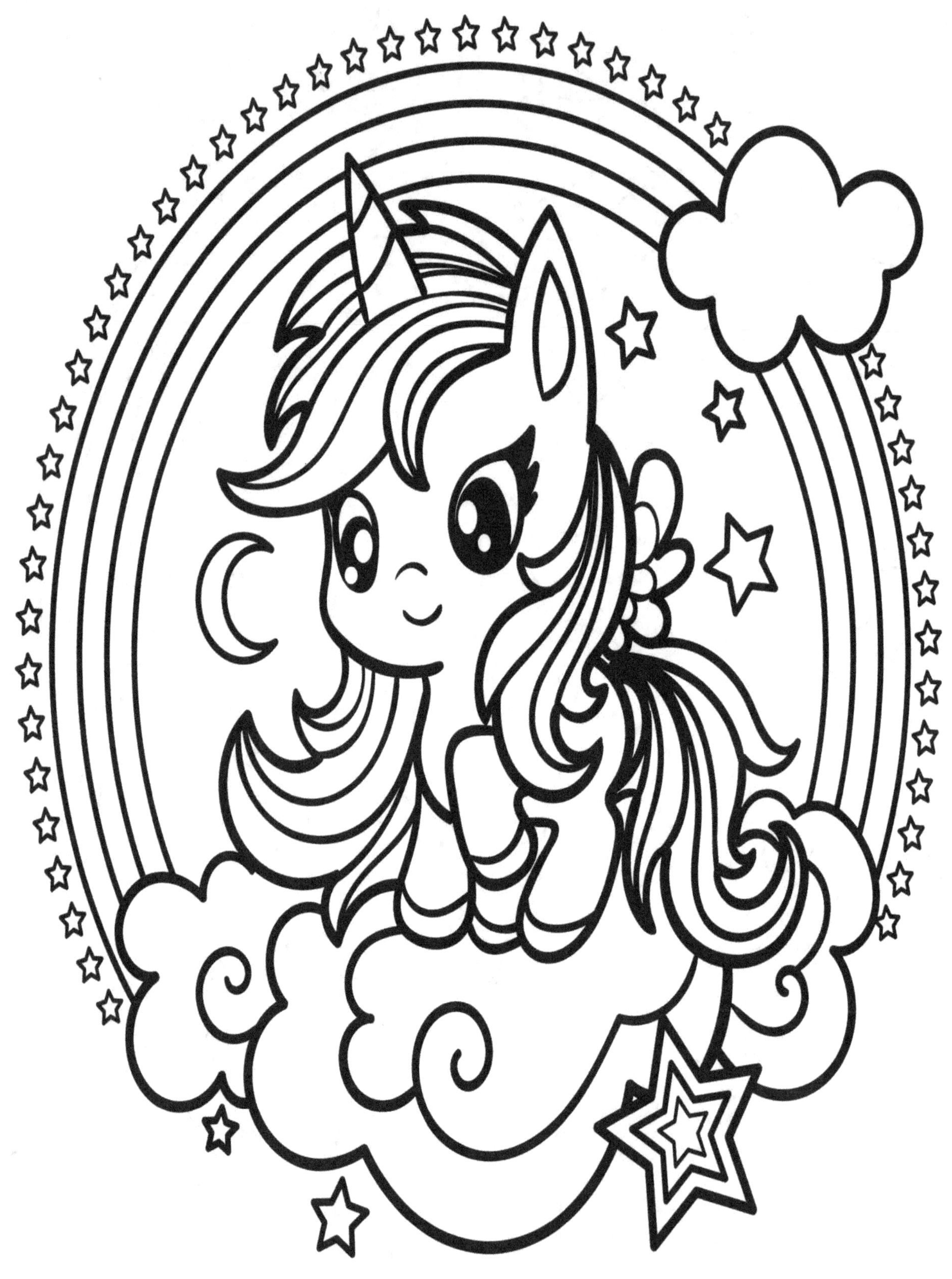

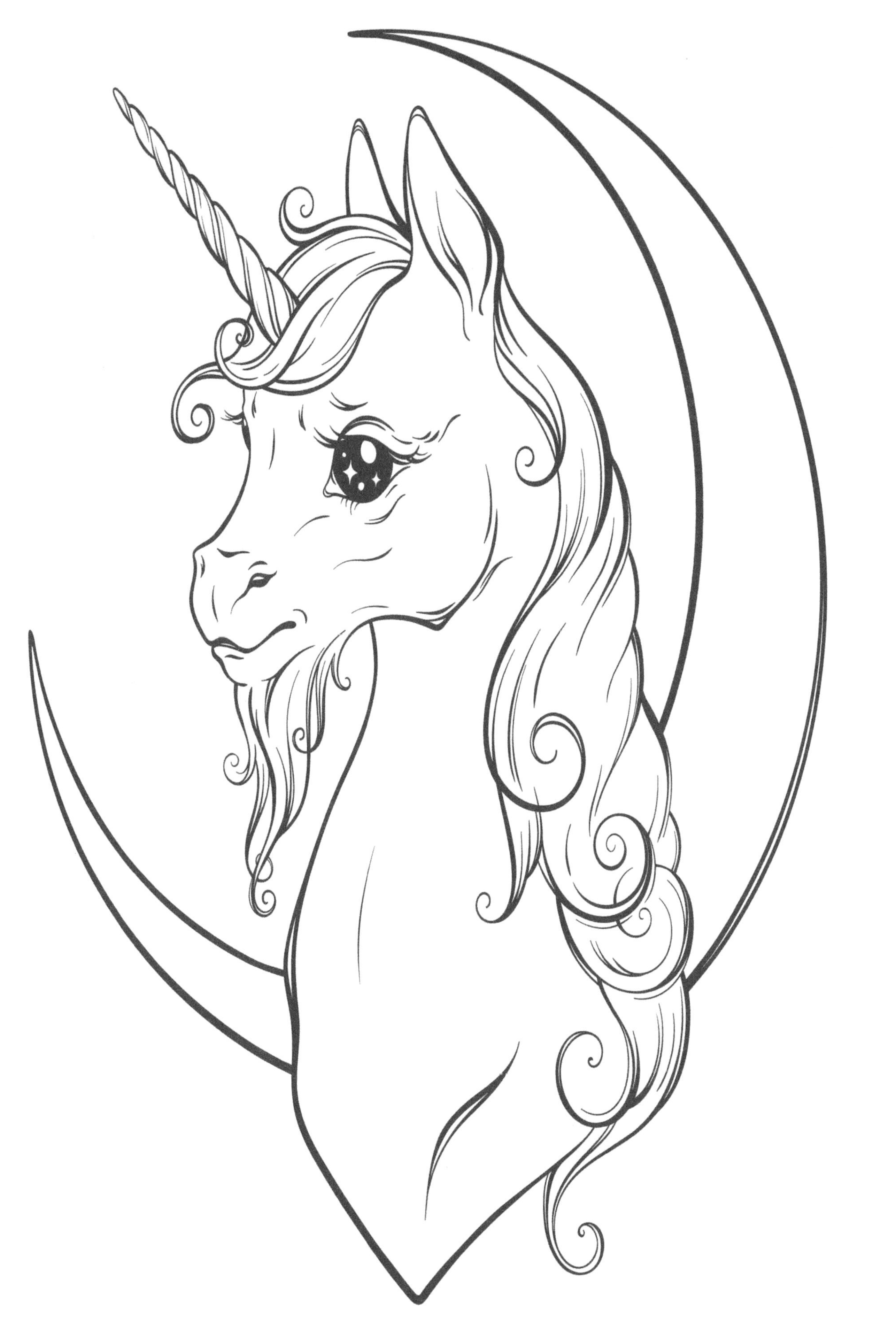

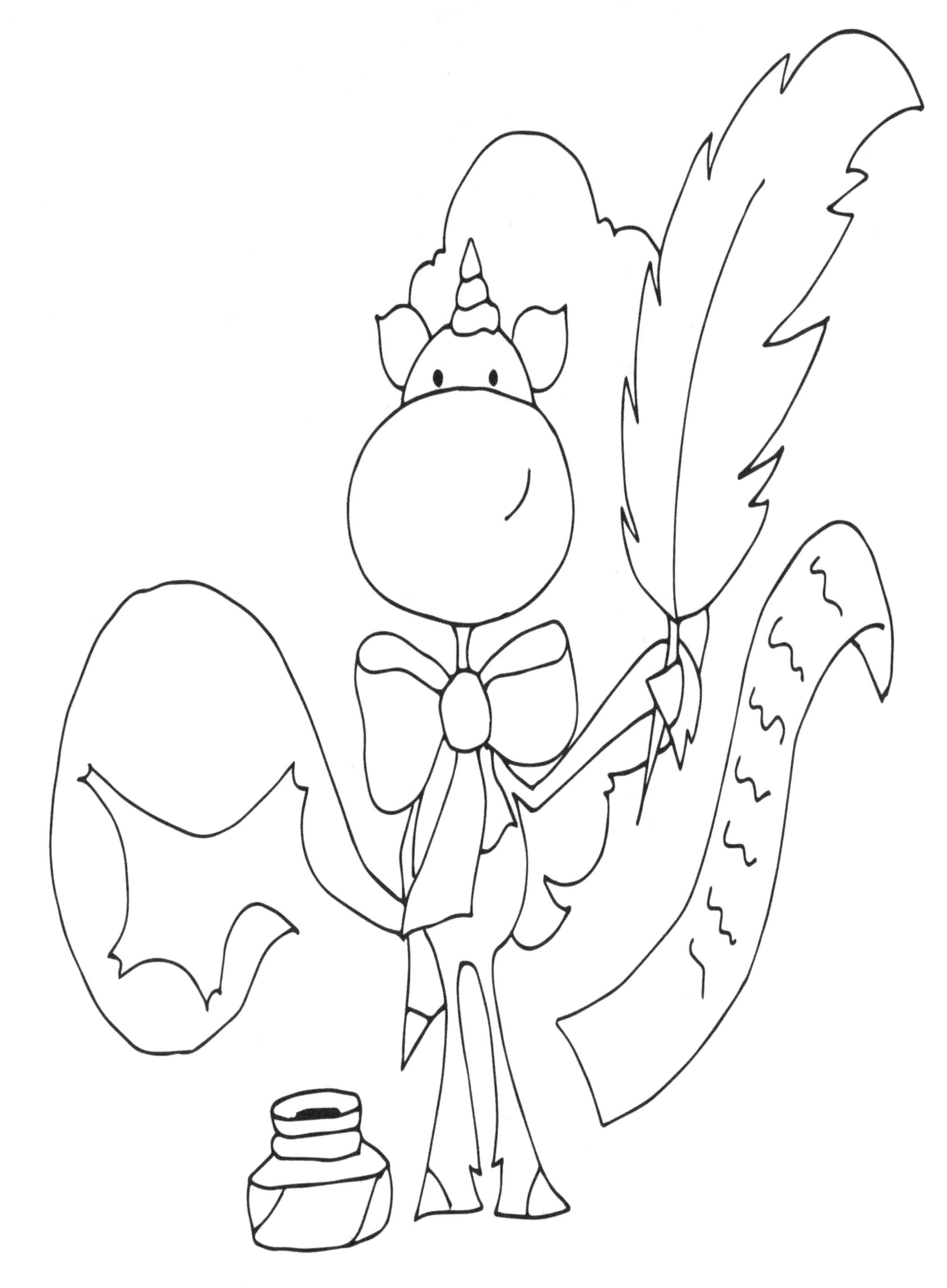

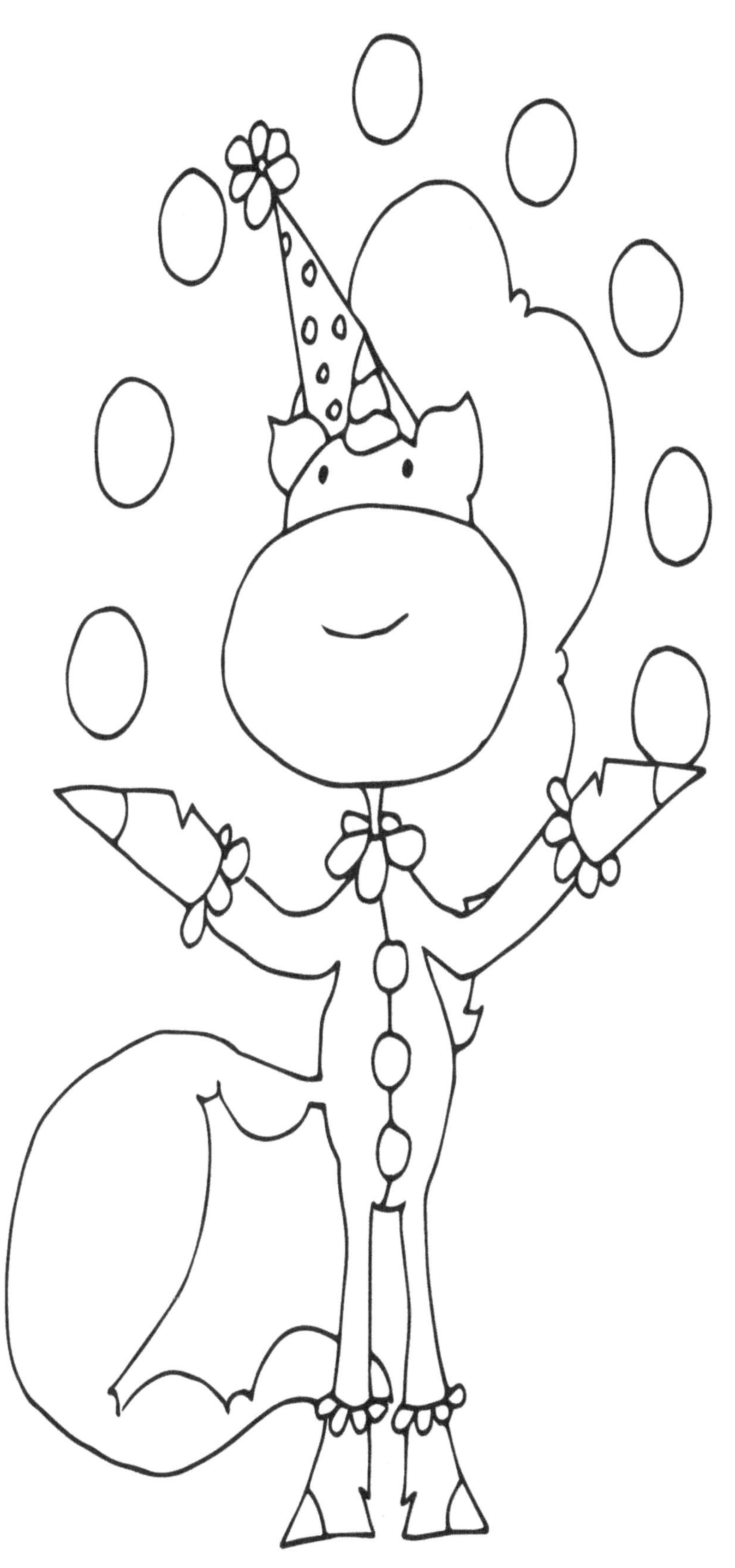

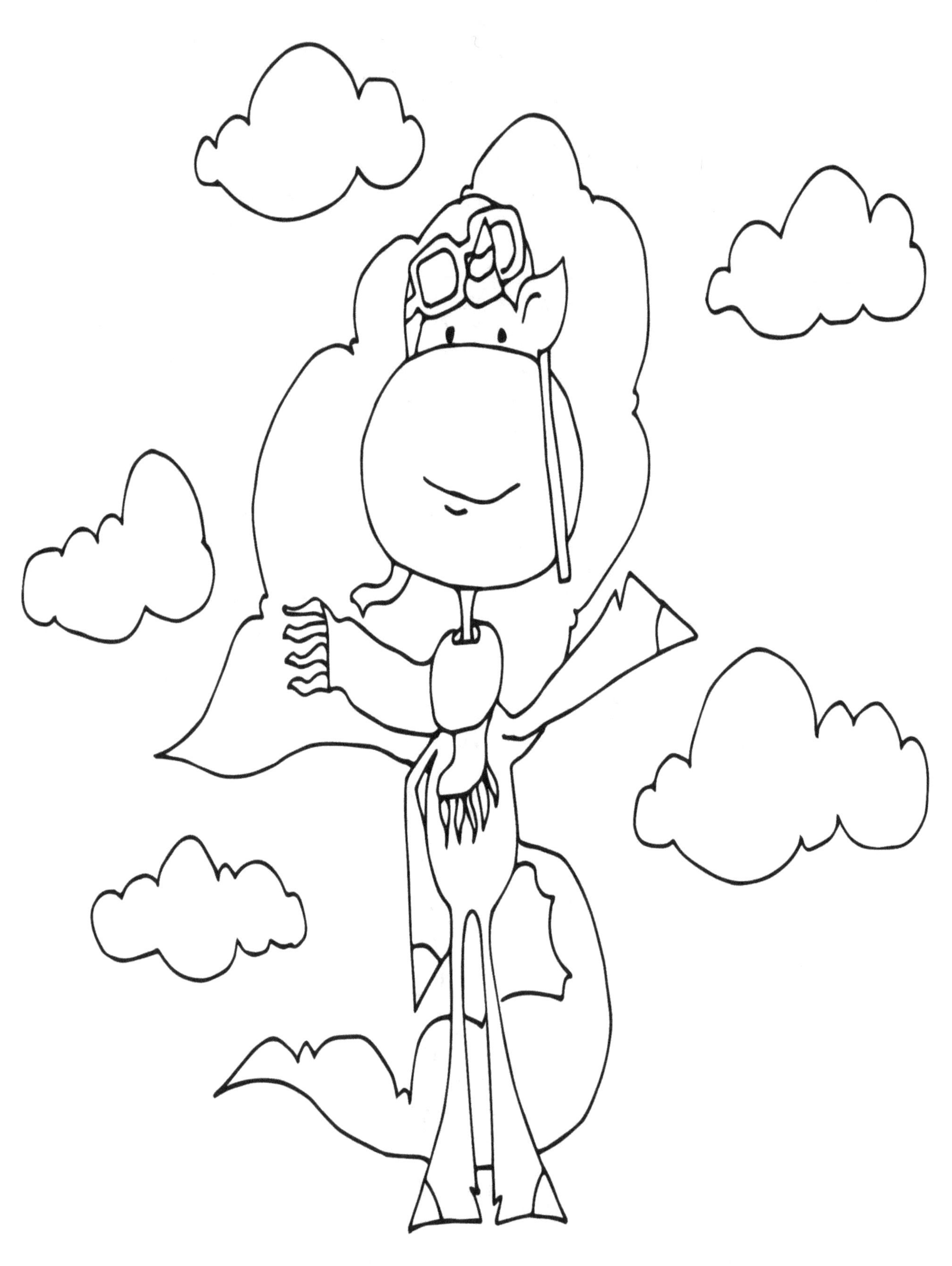

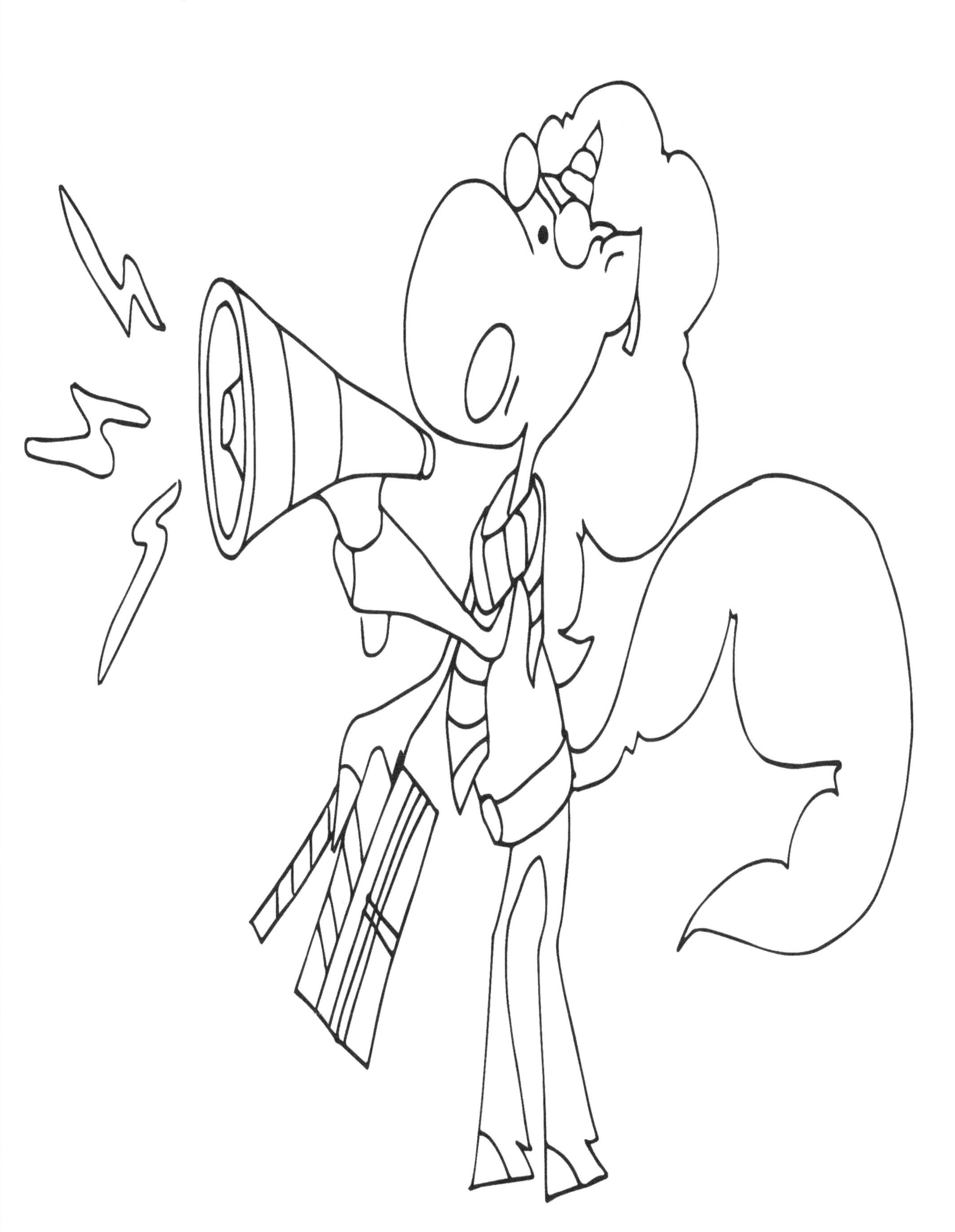

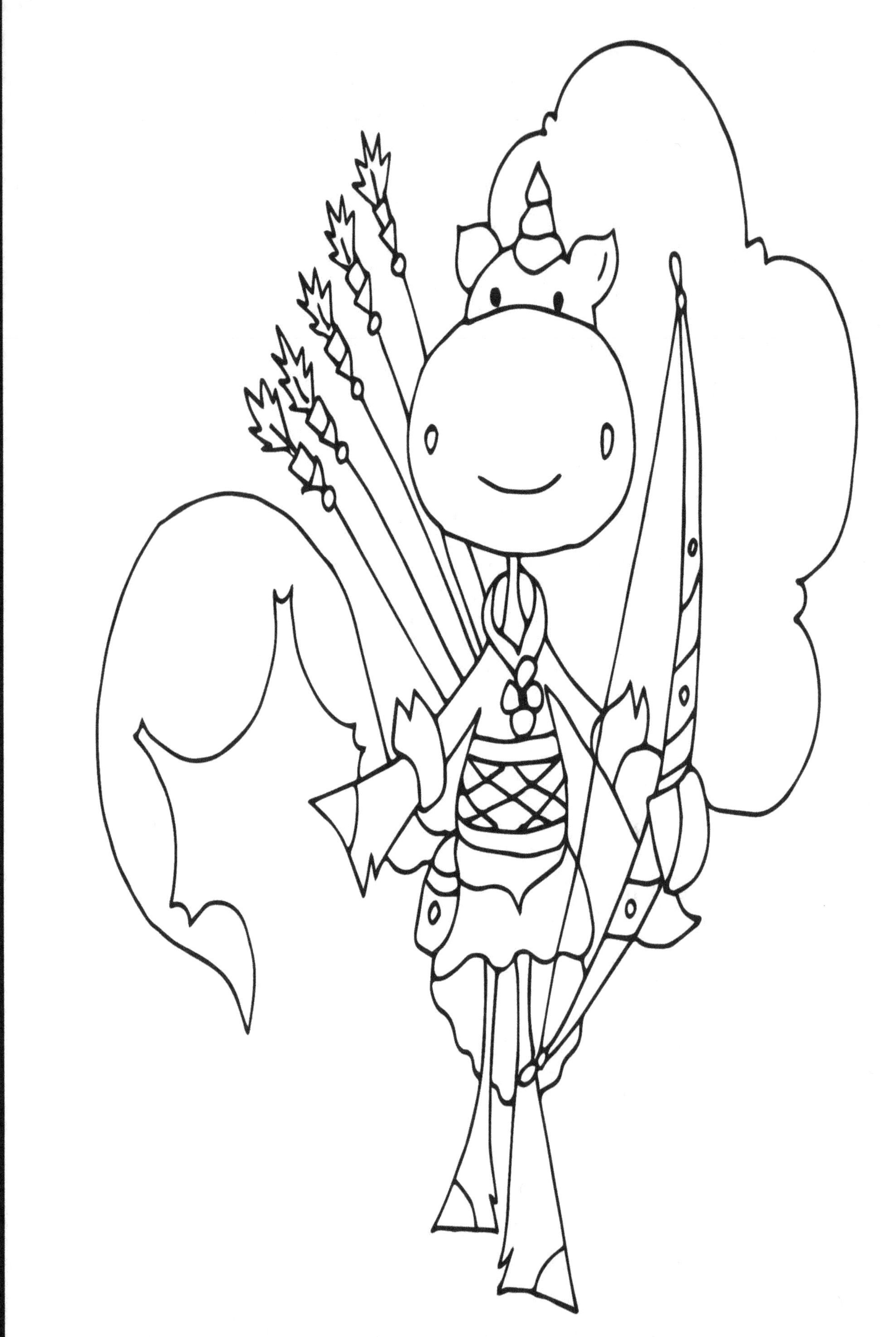

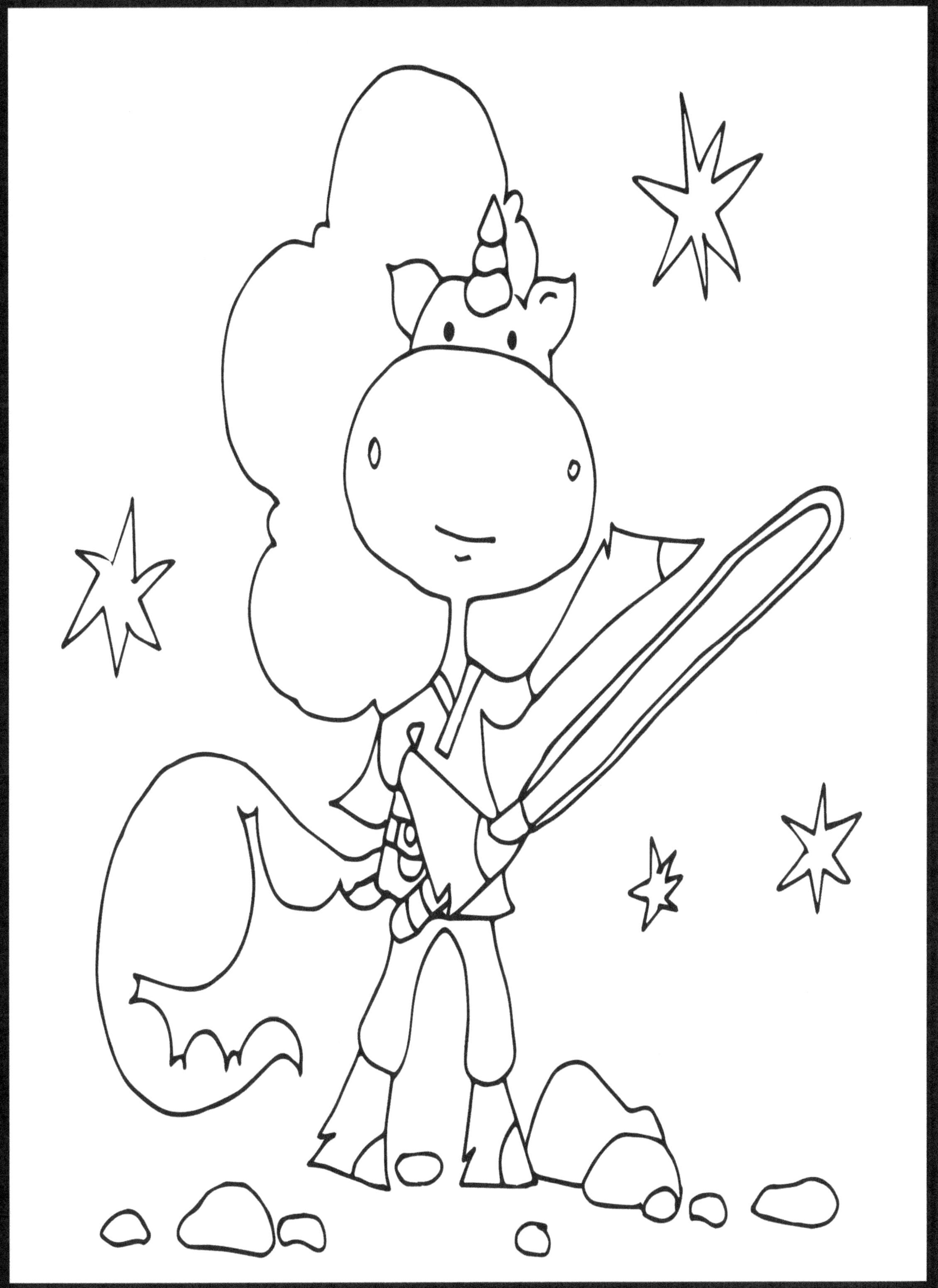

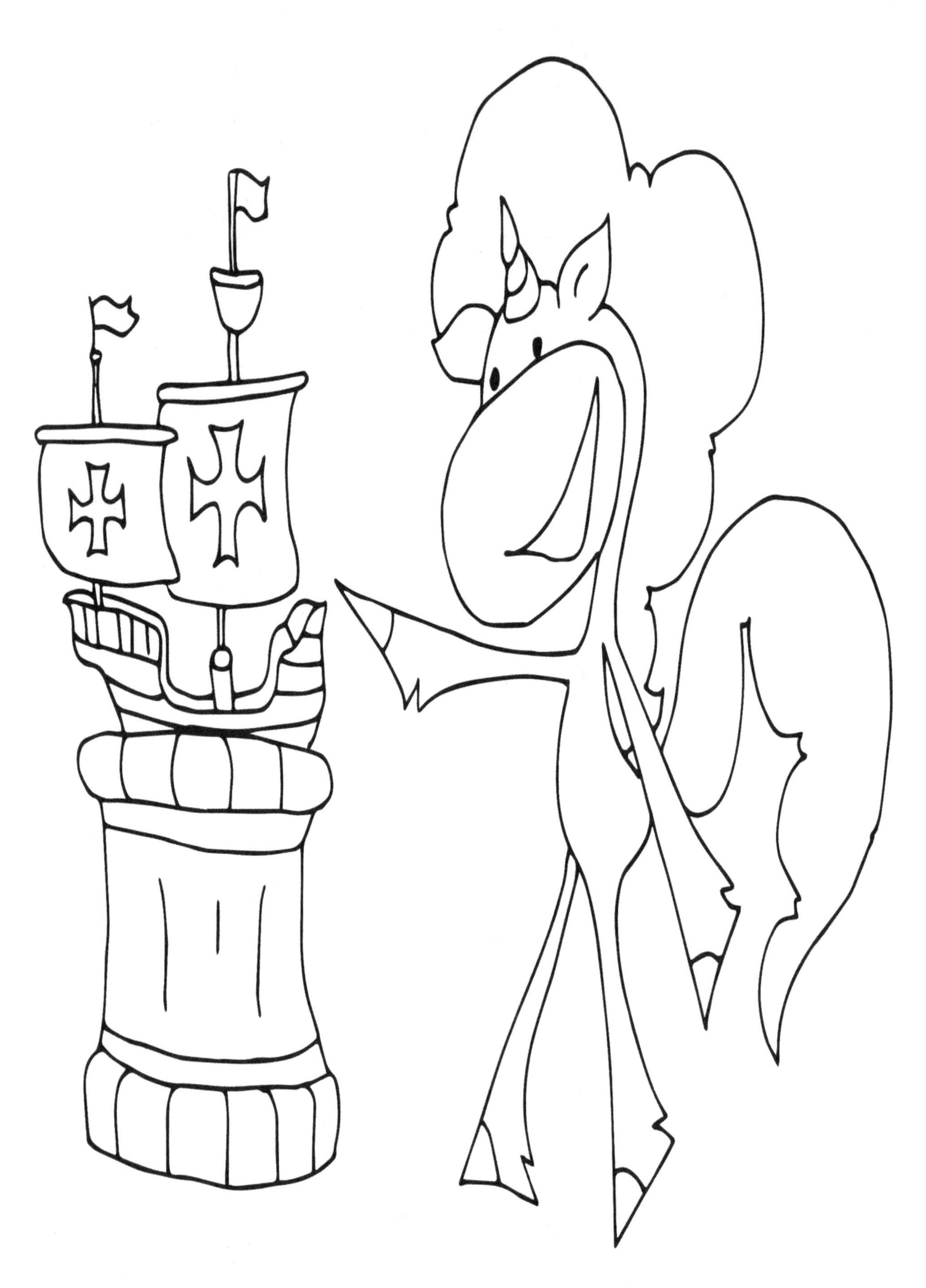

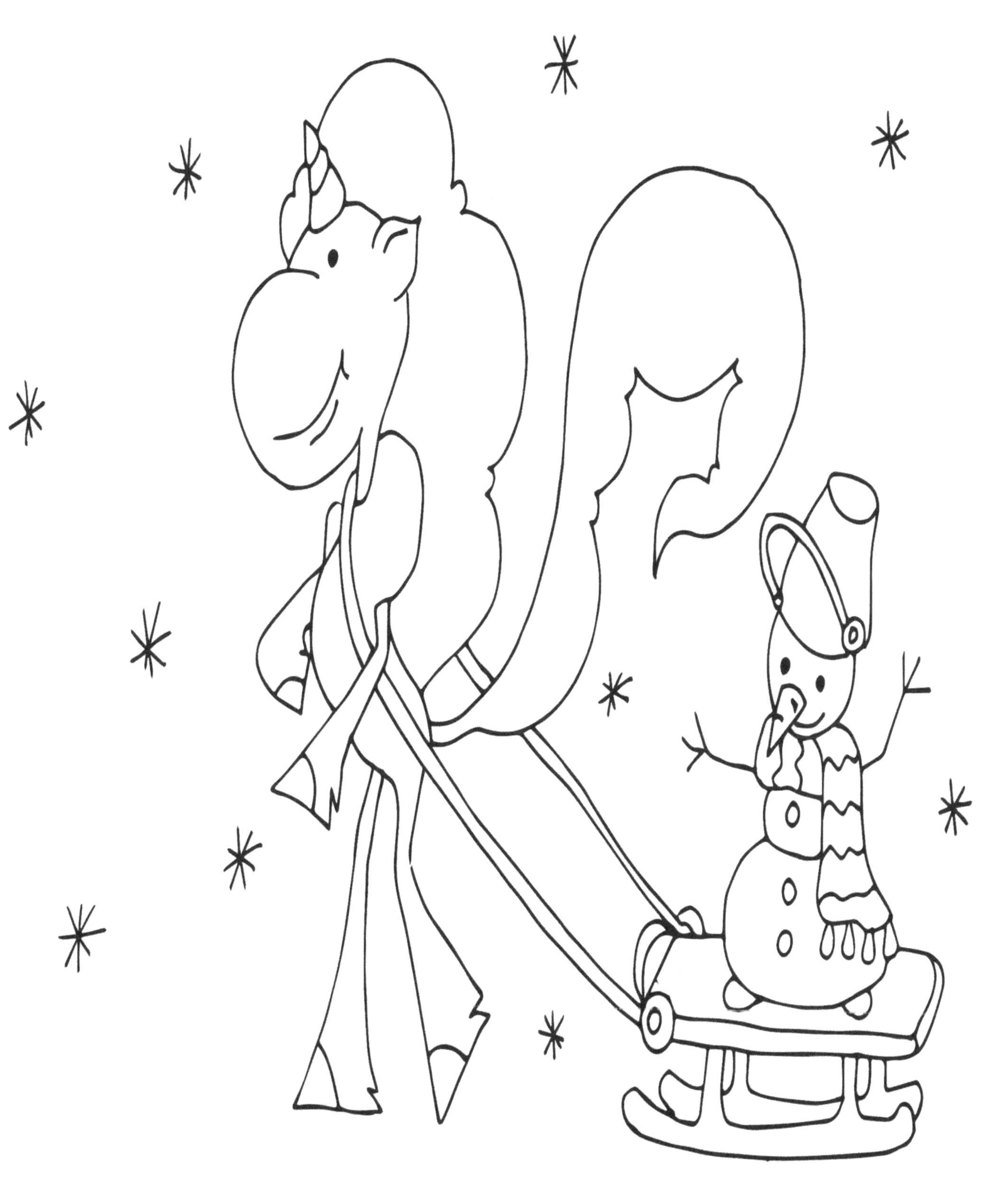

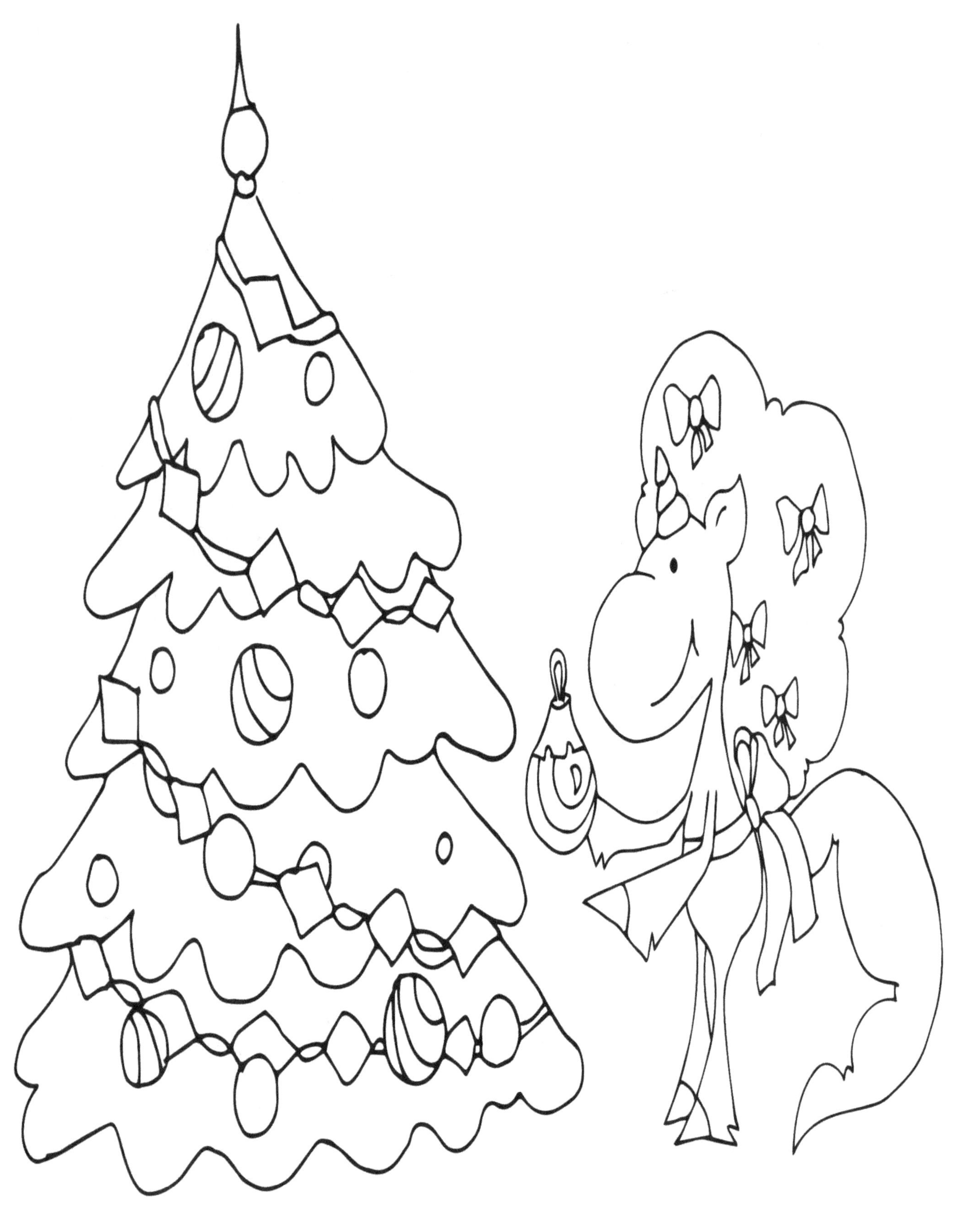

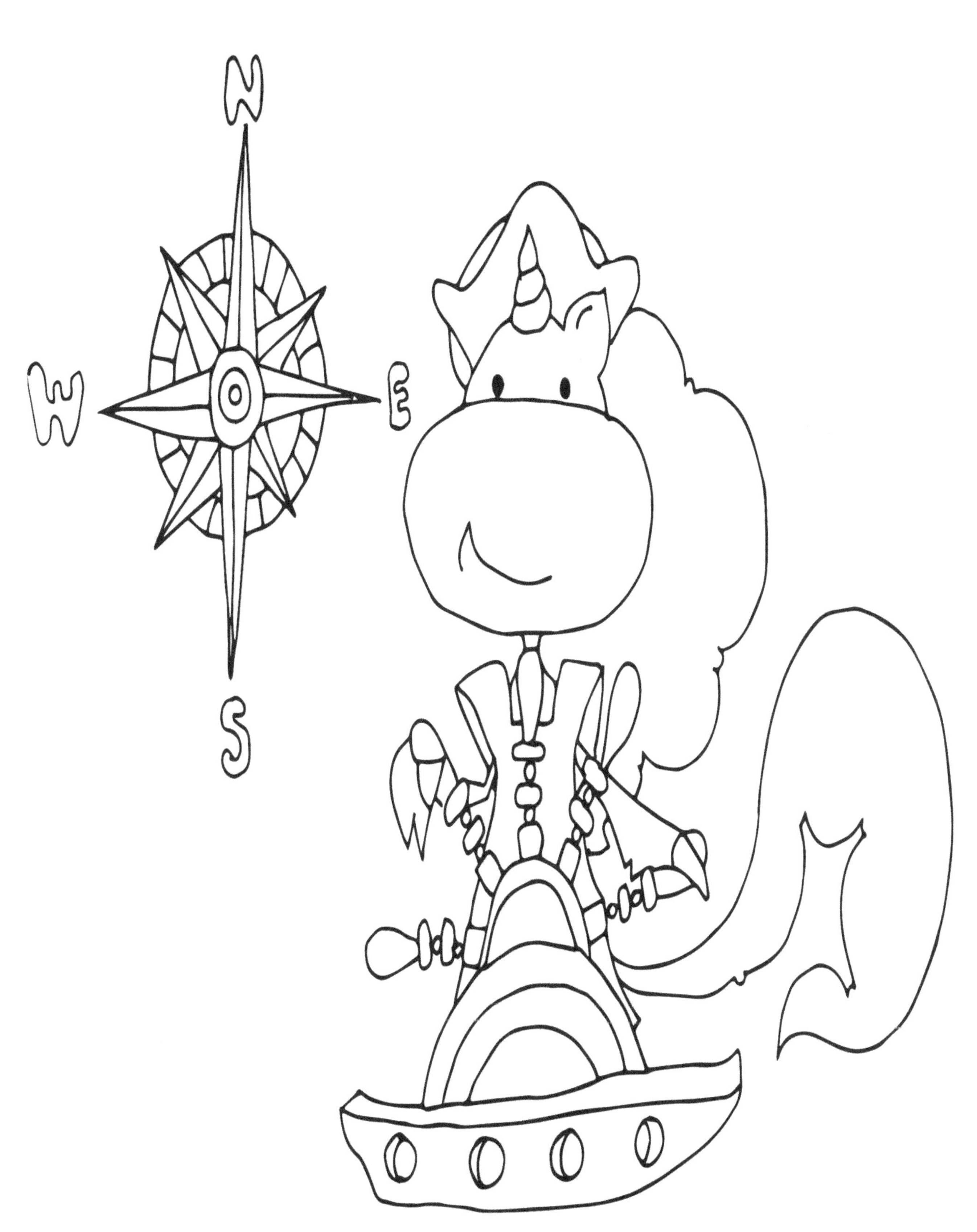

N
W
E
S

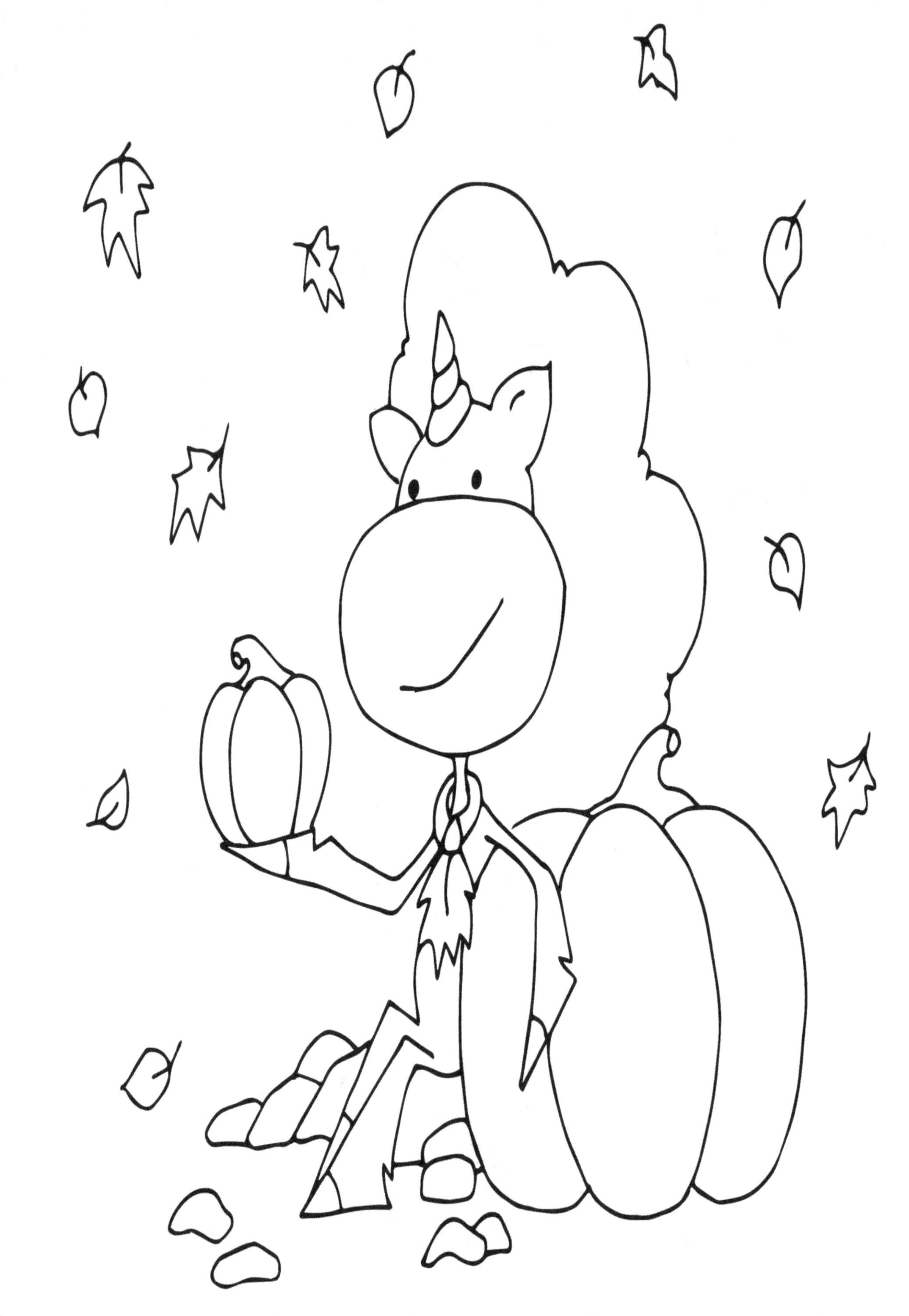

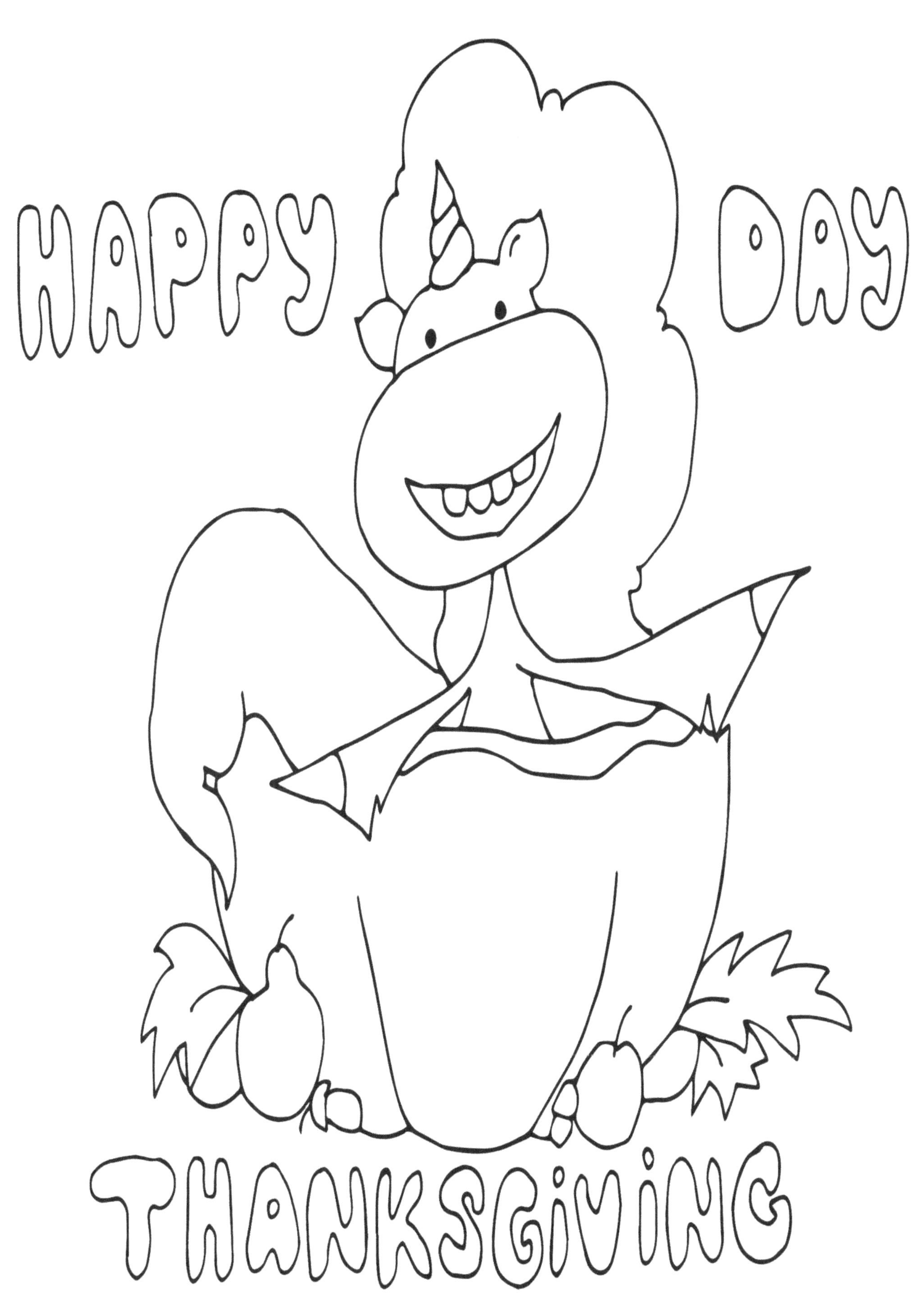

HAPPY
DAY
THANKSGIVING

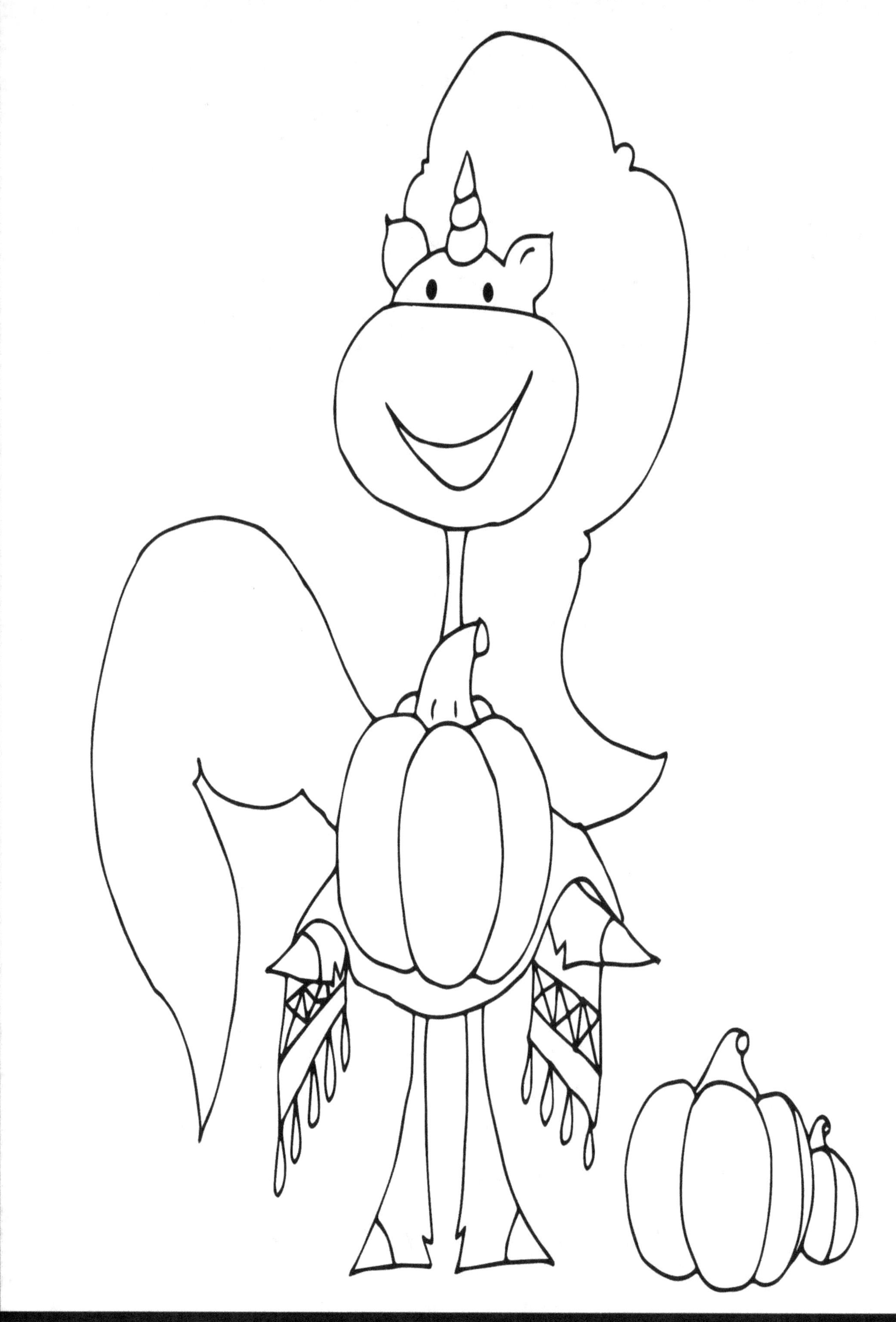

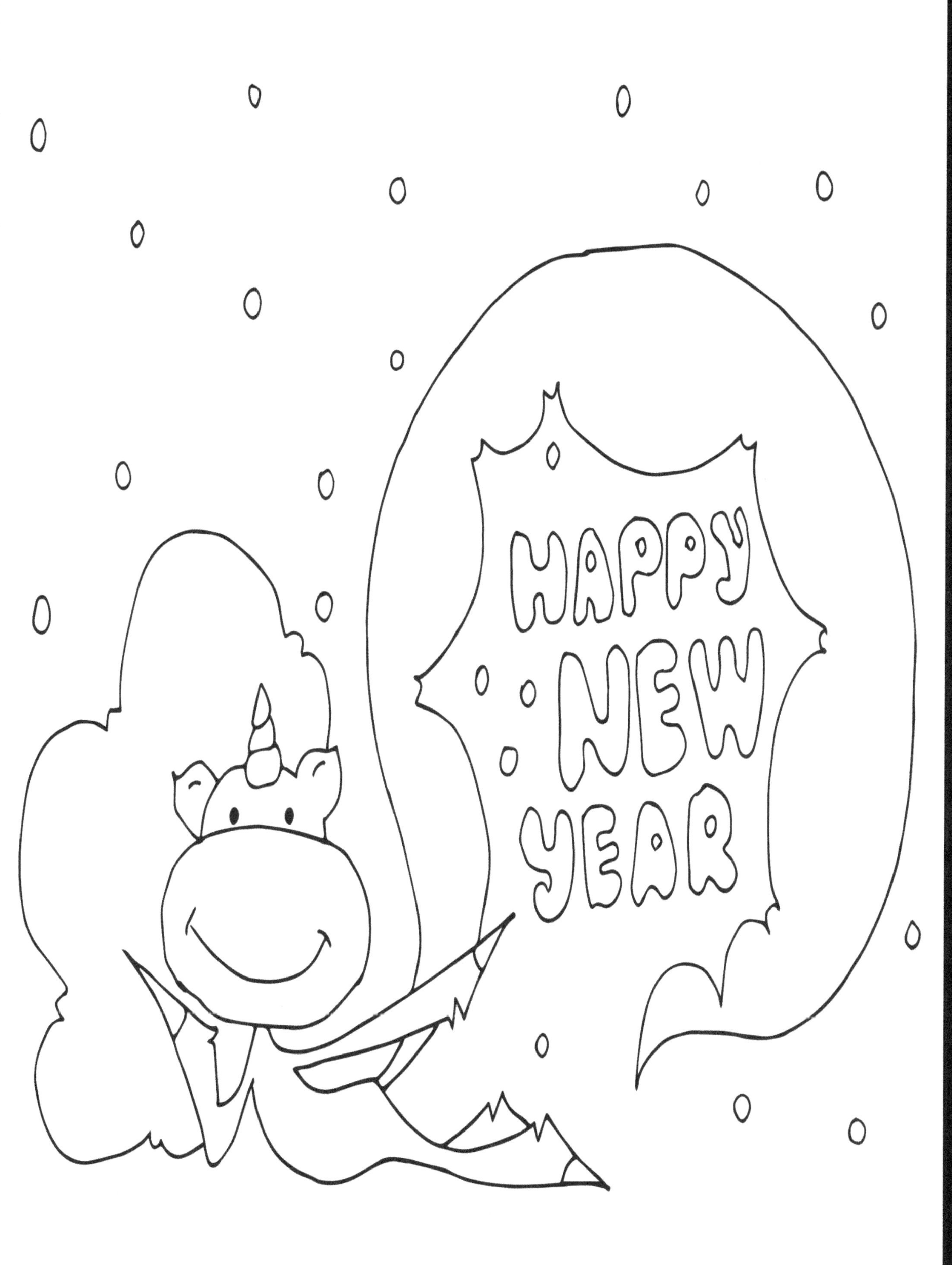

HAPPY
NEW
YEAR

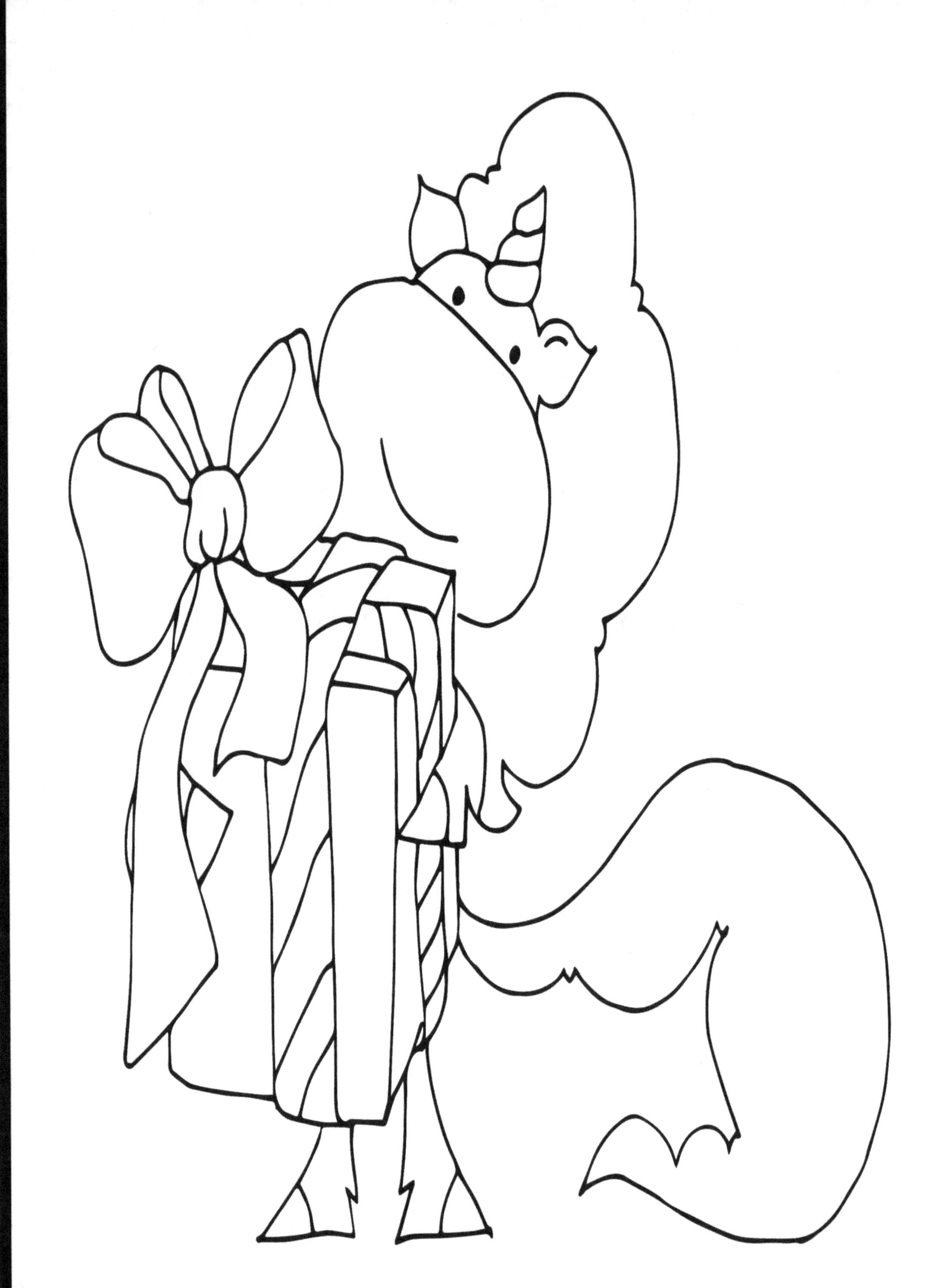

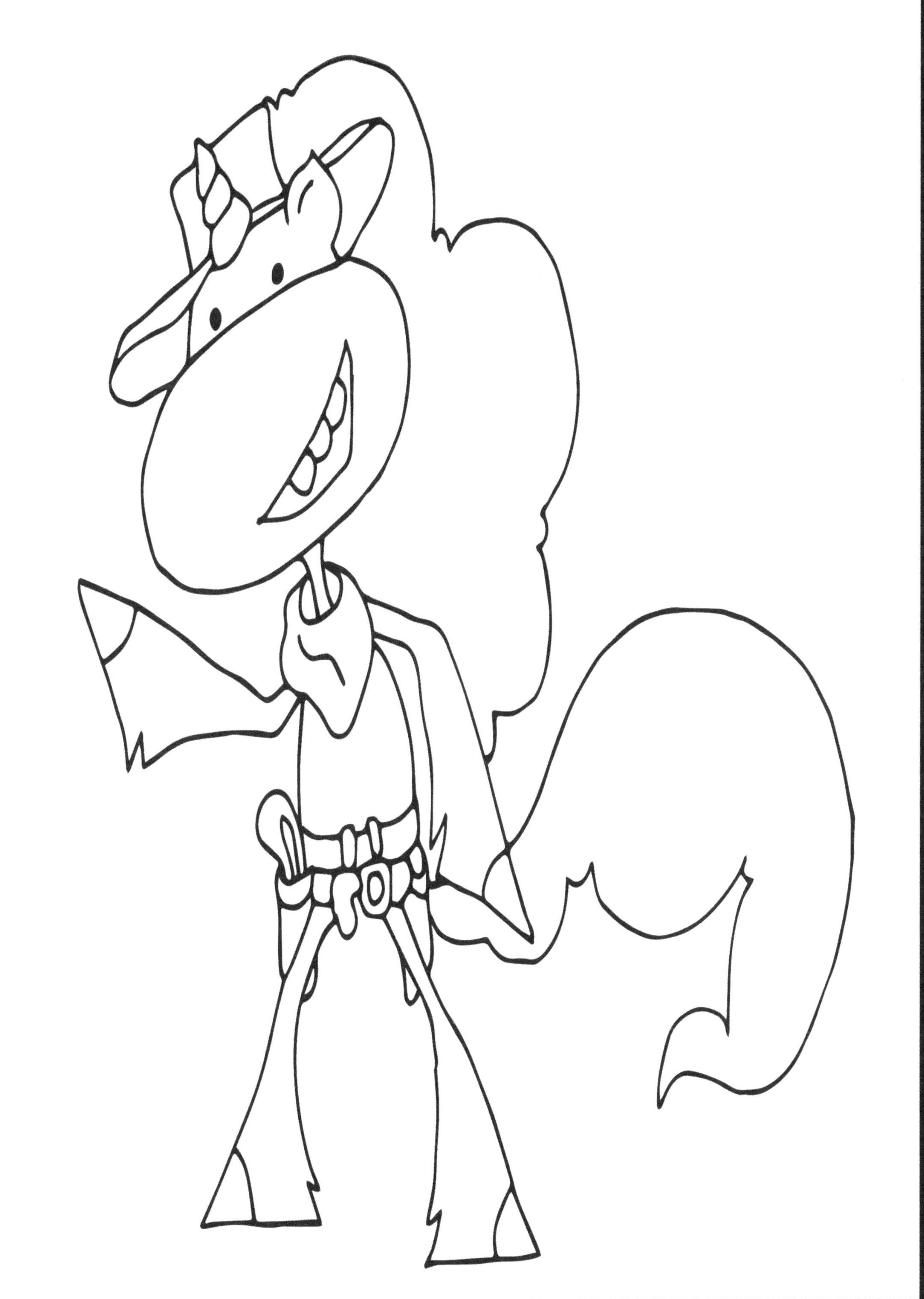

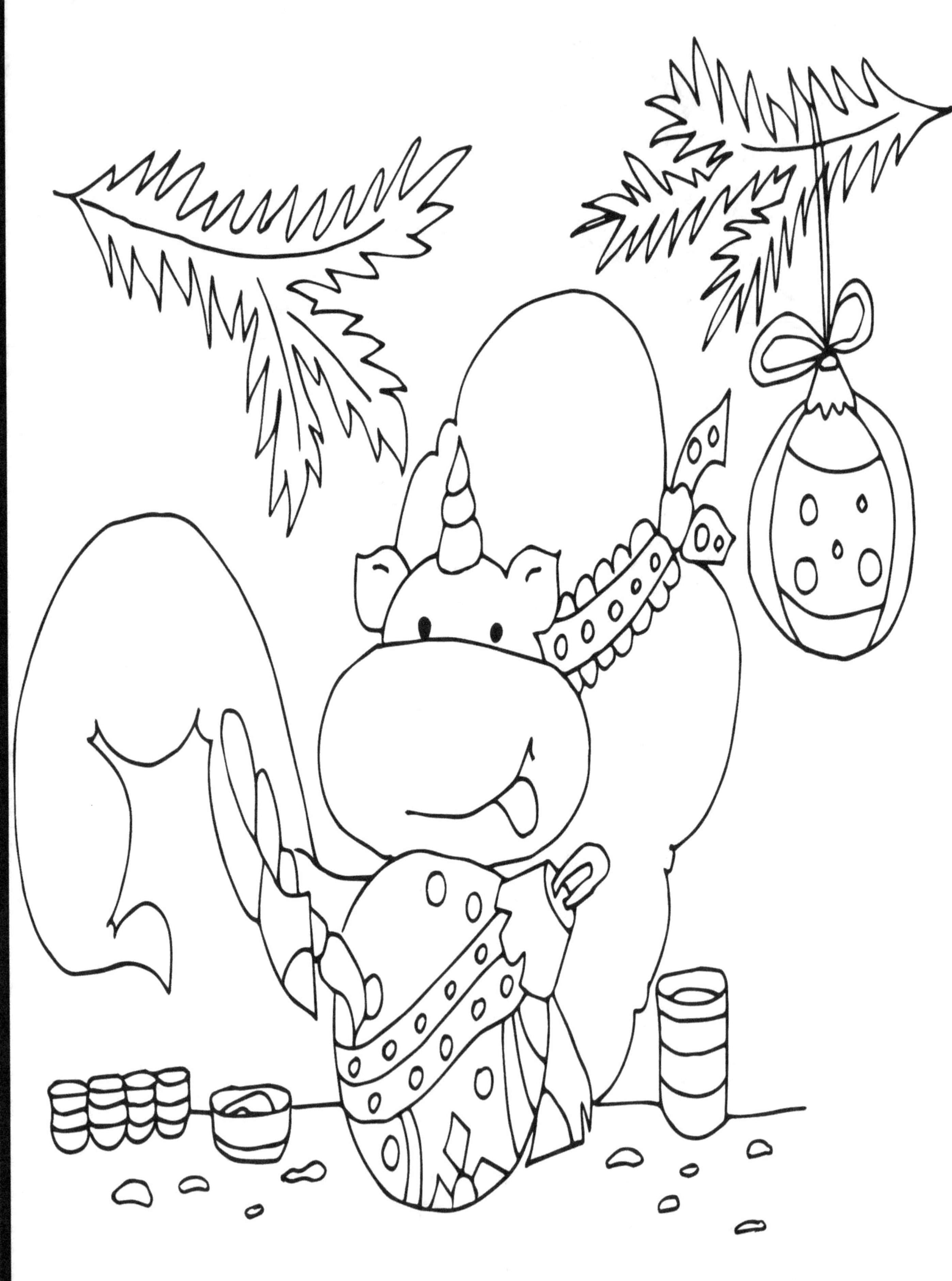

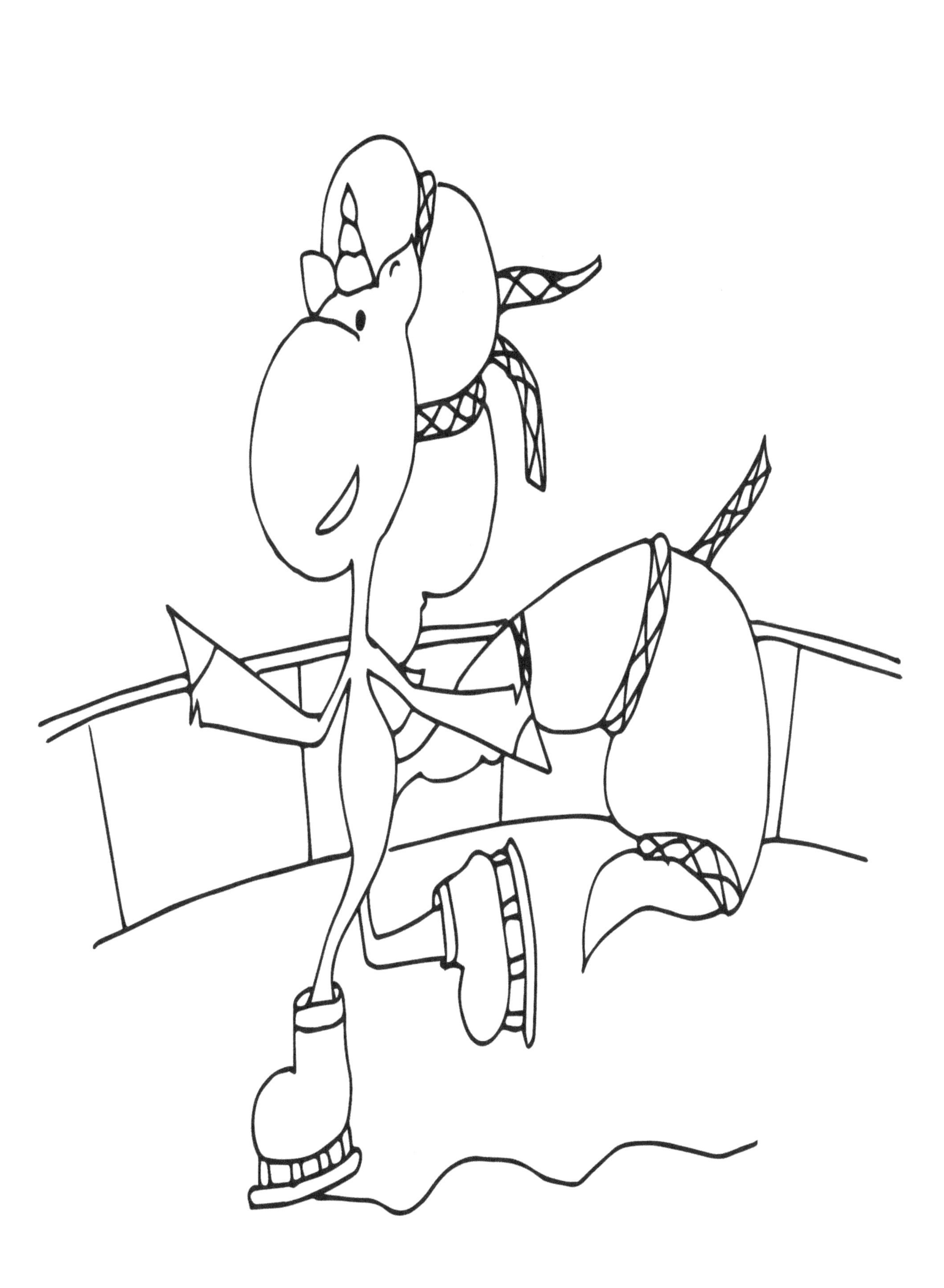

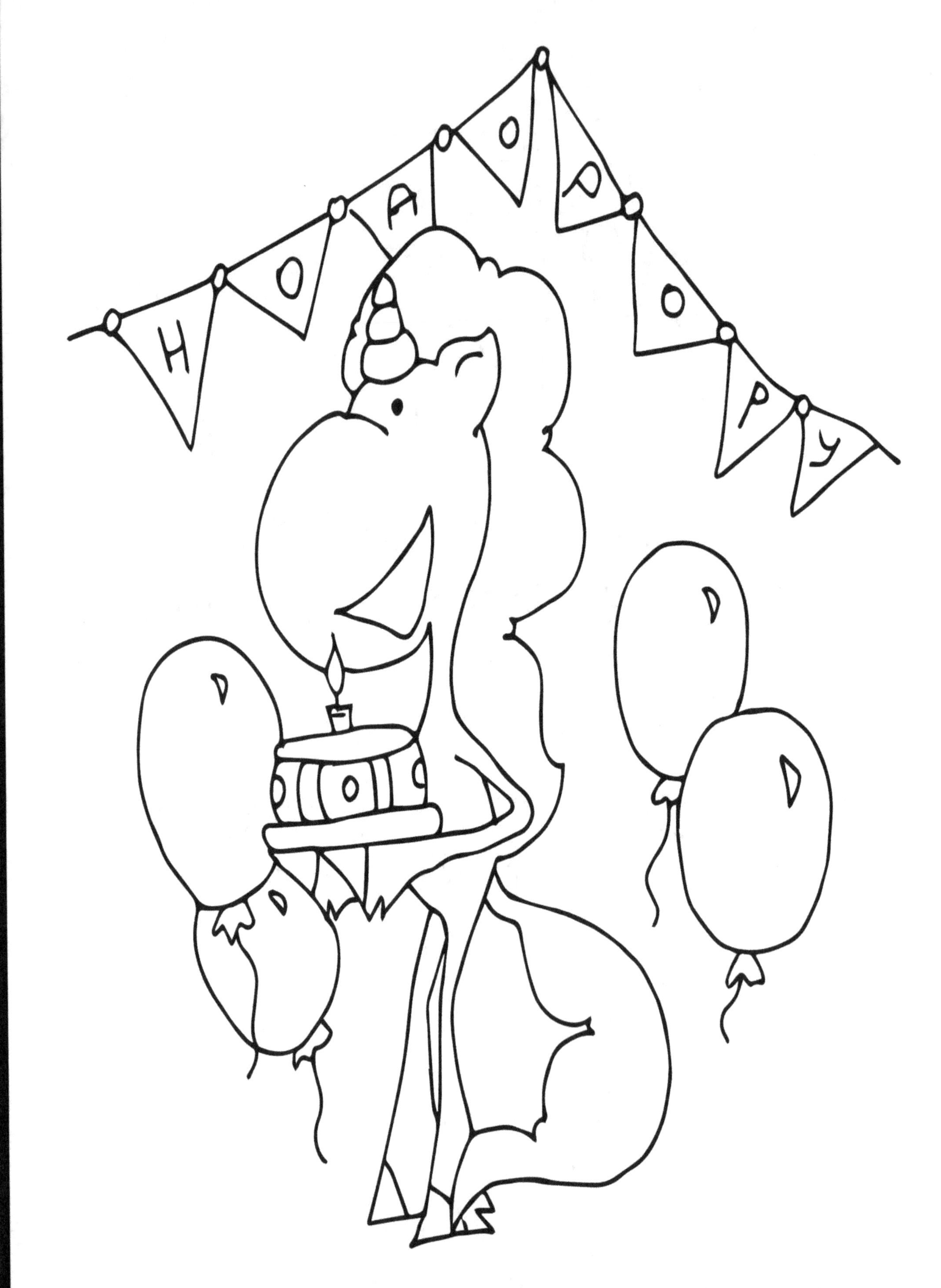

HAPPY

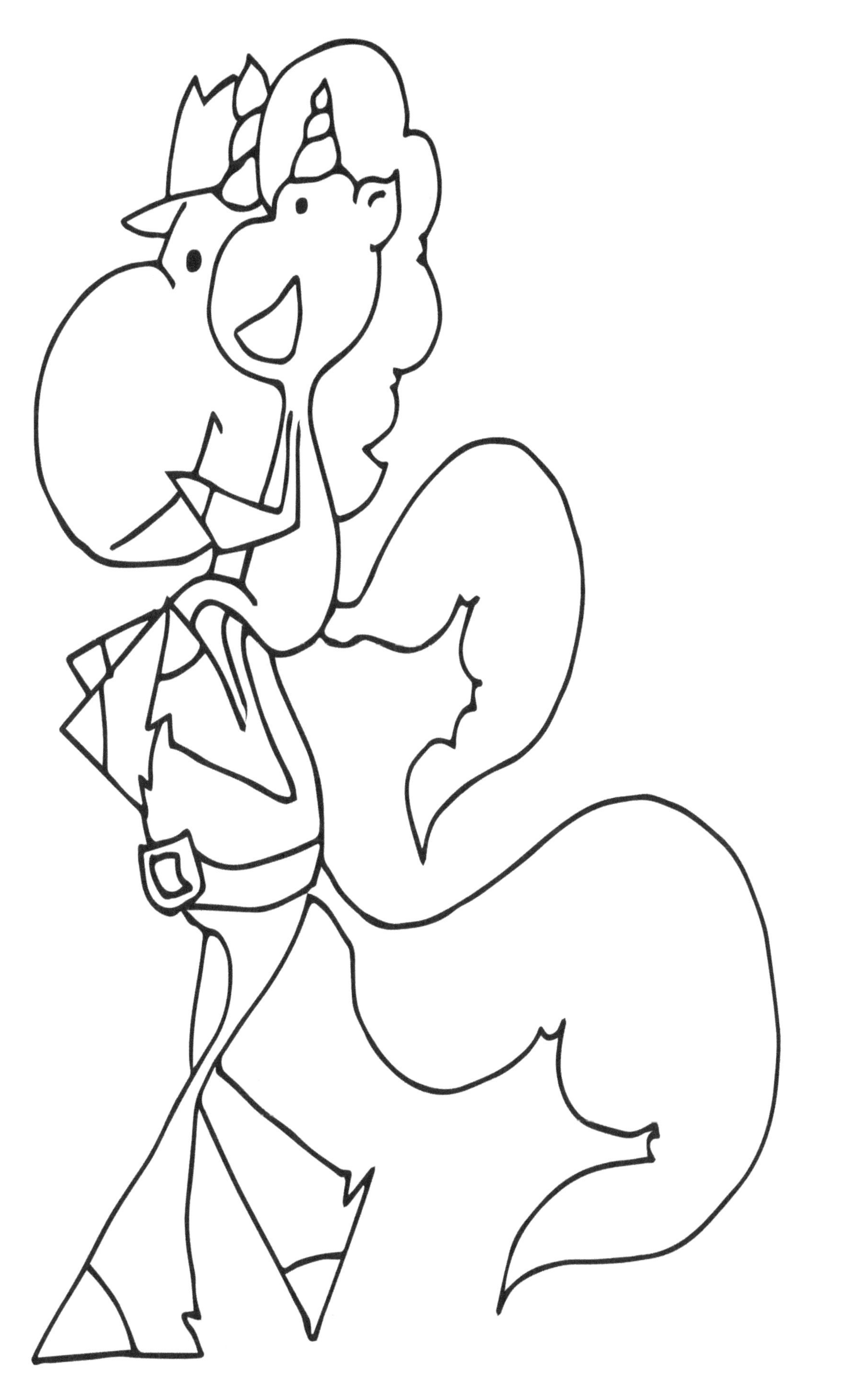

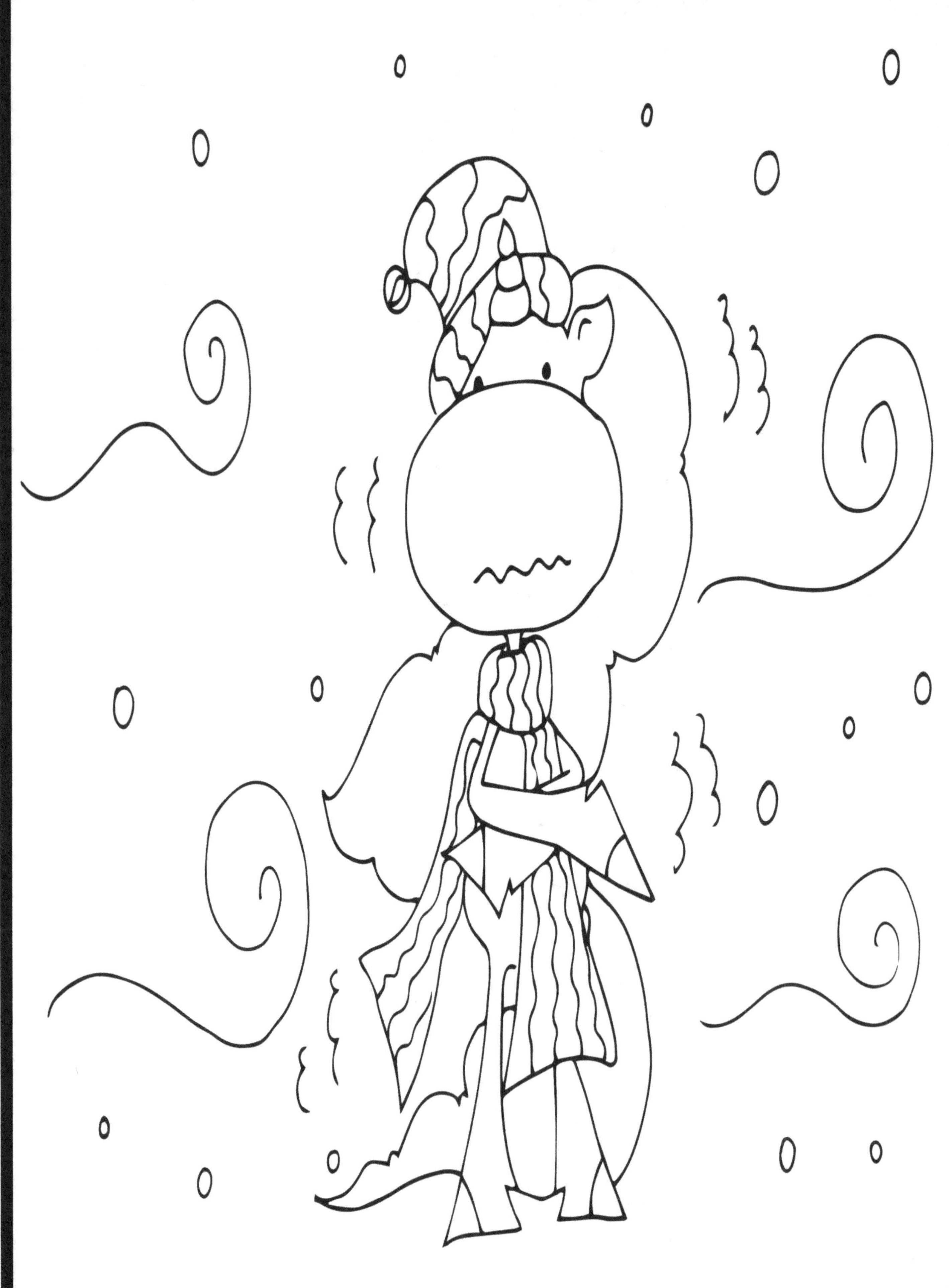

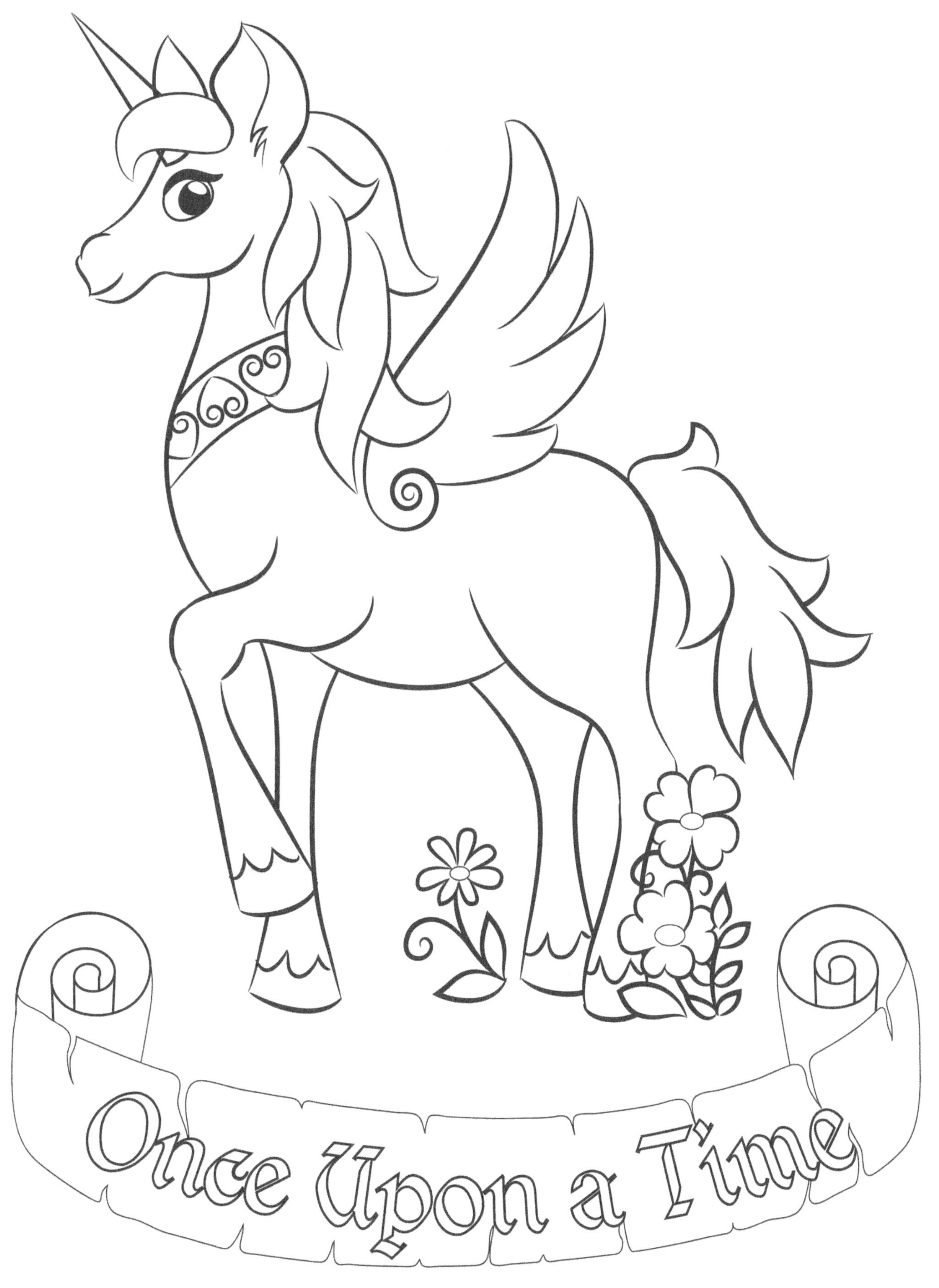

Once Upon a Time

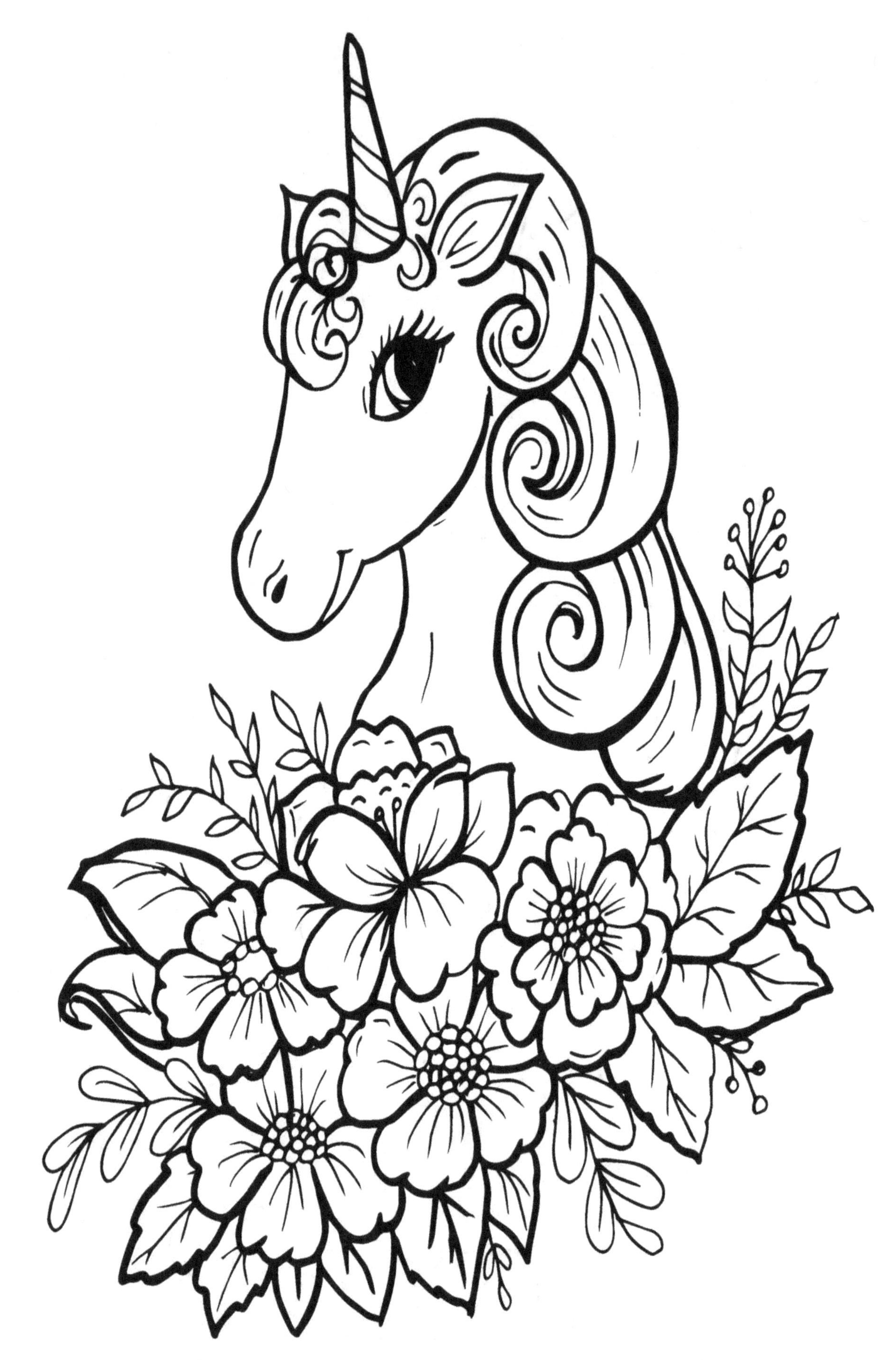

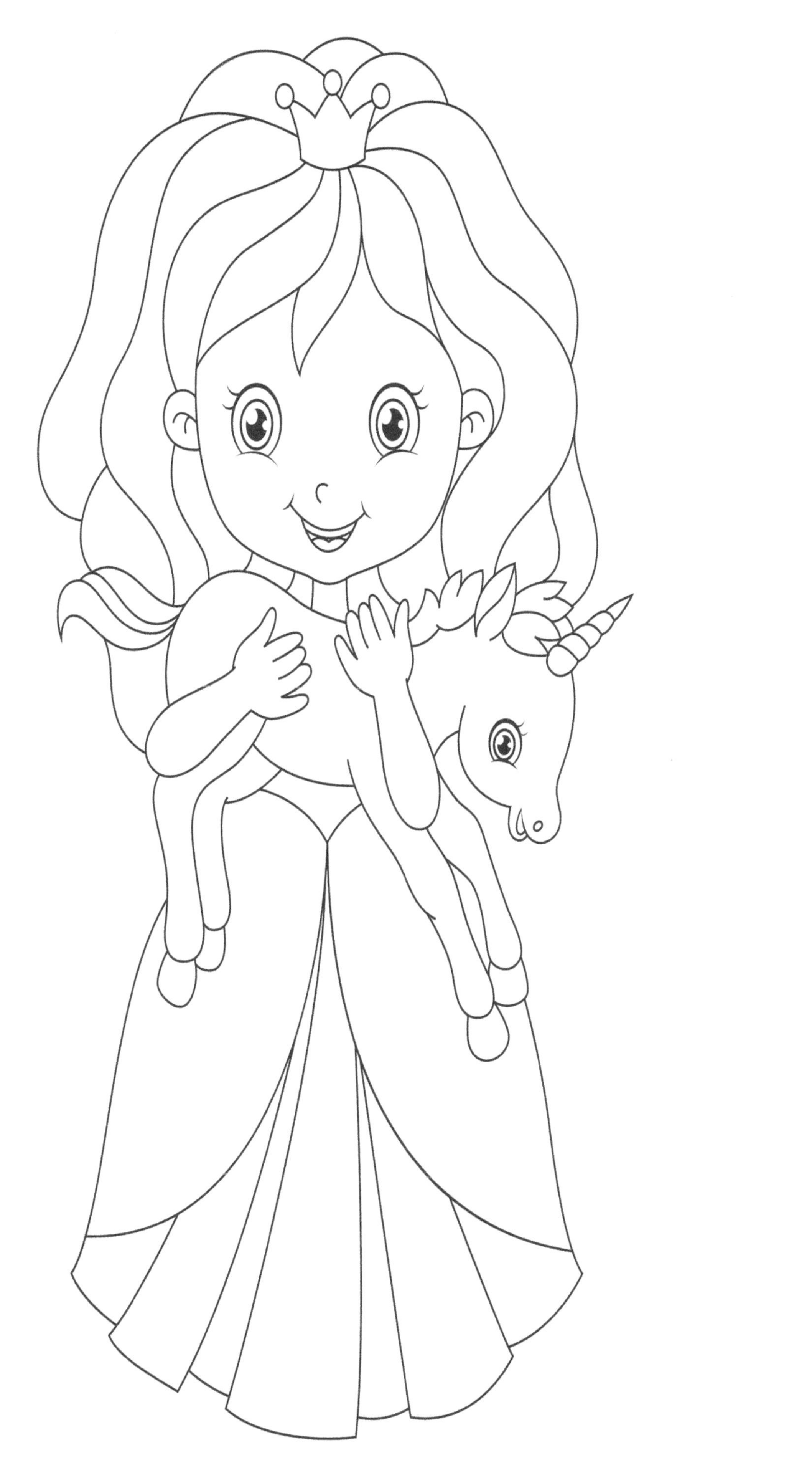

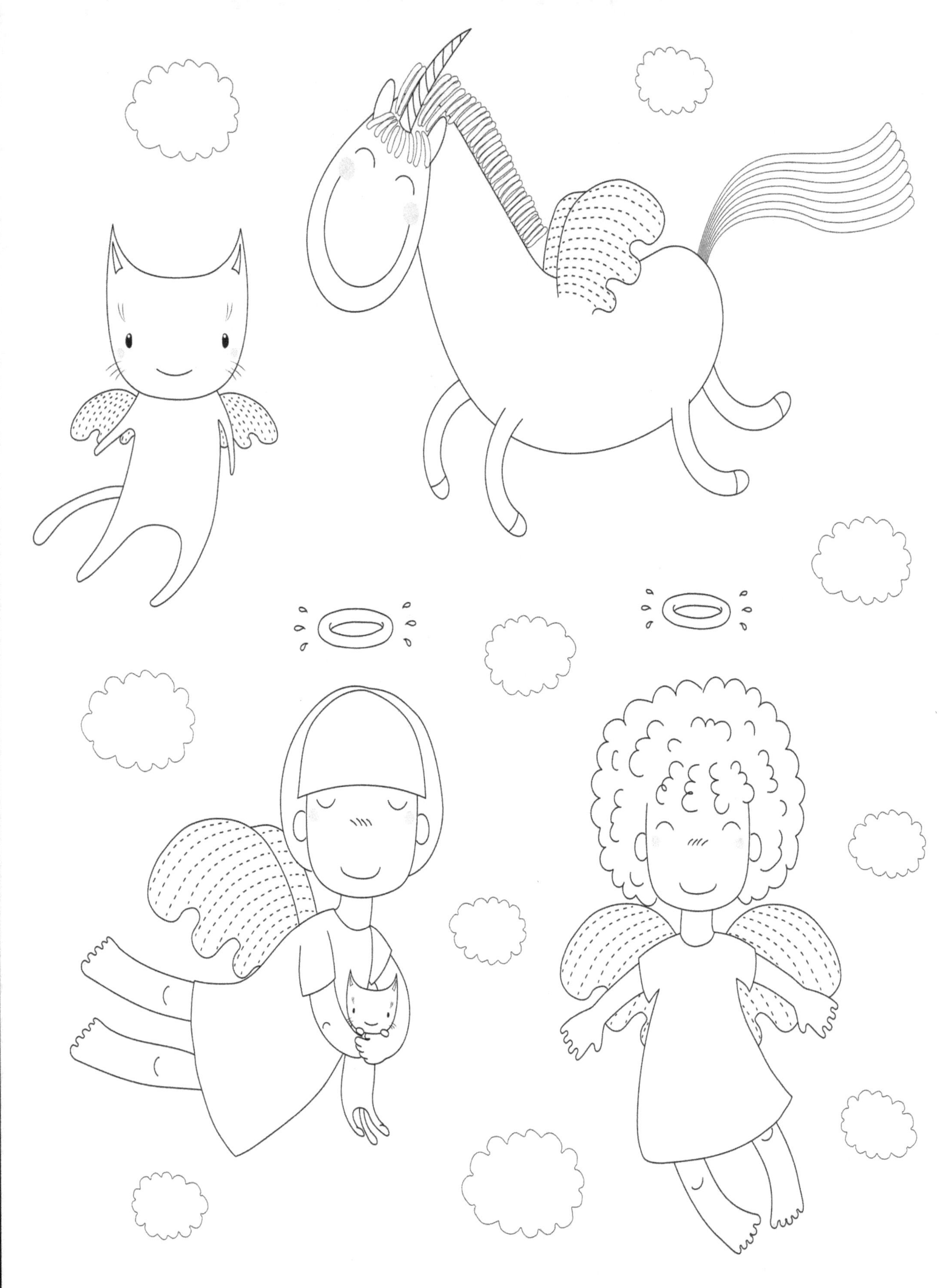

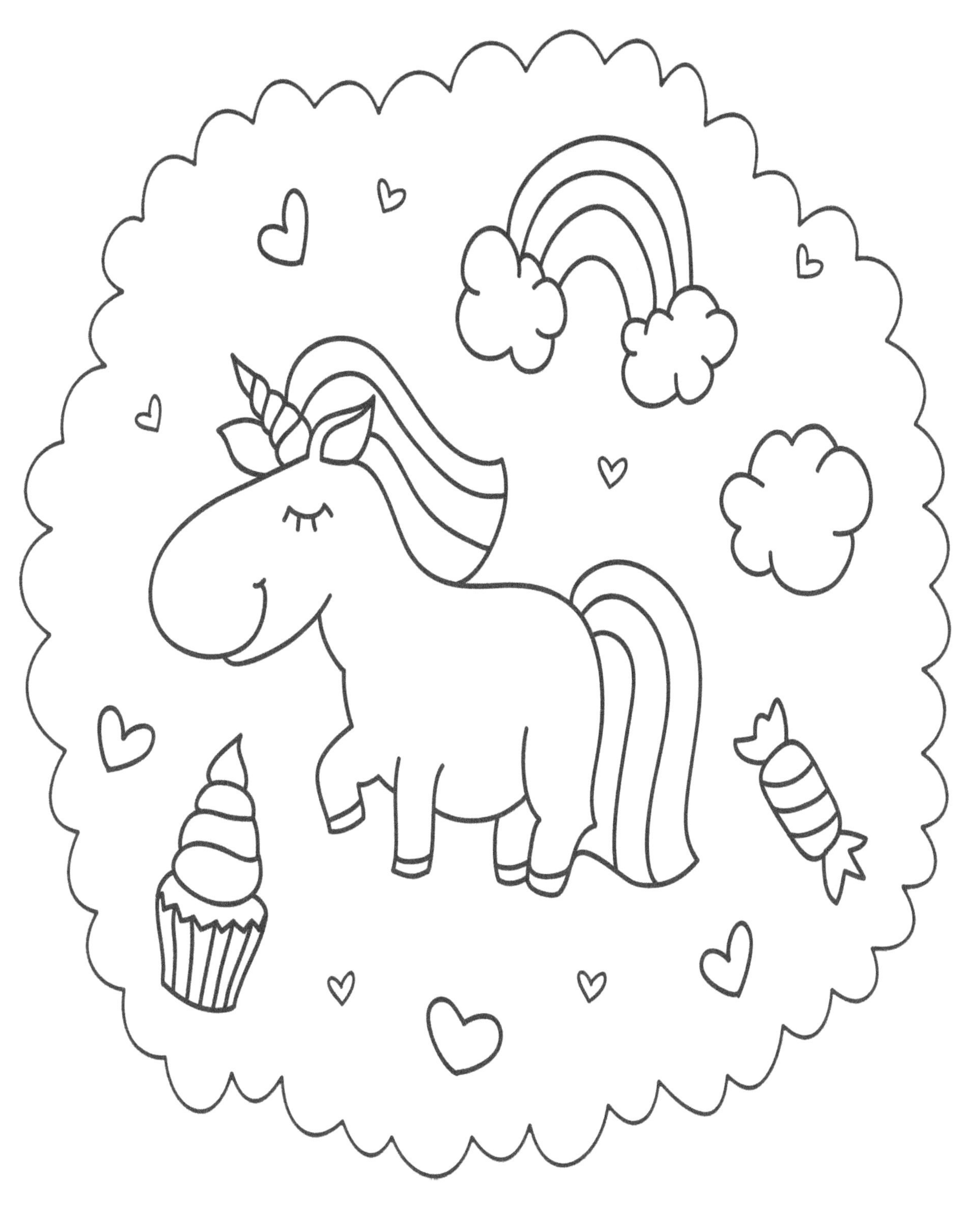

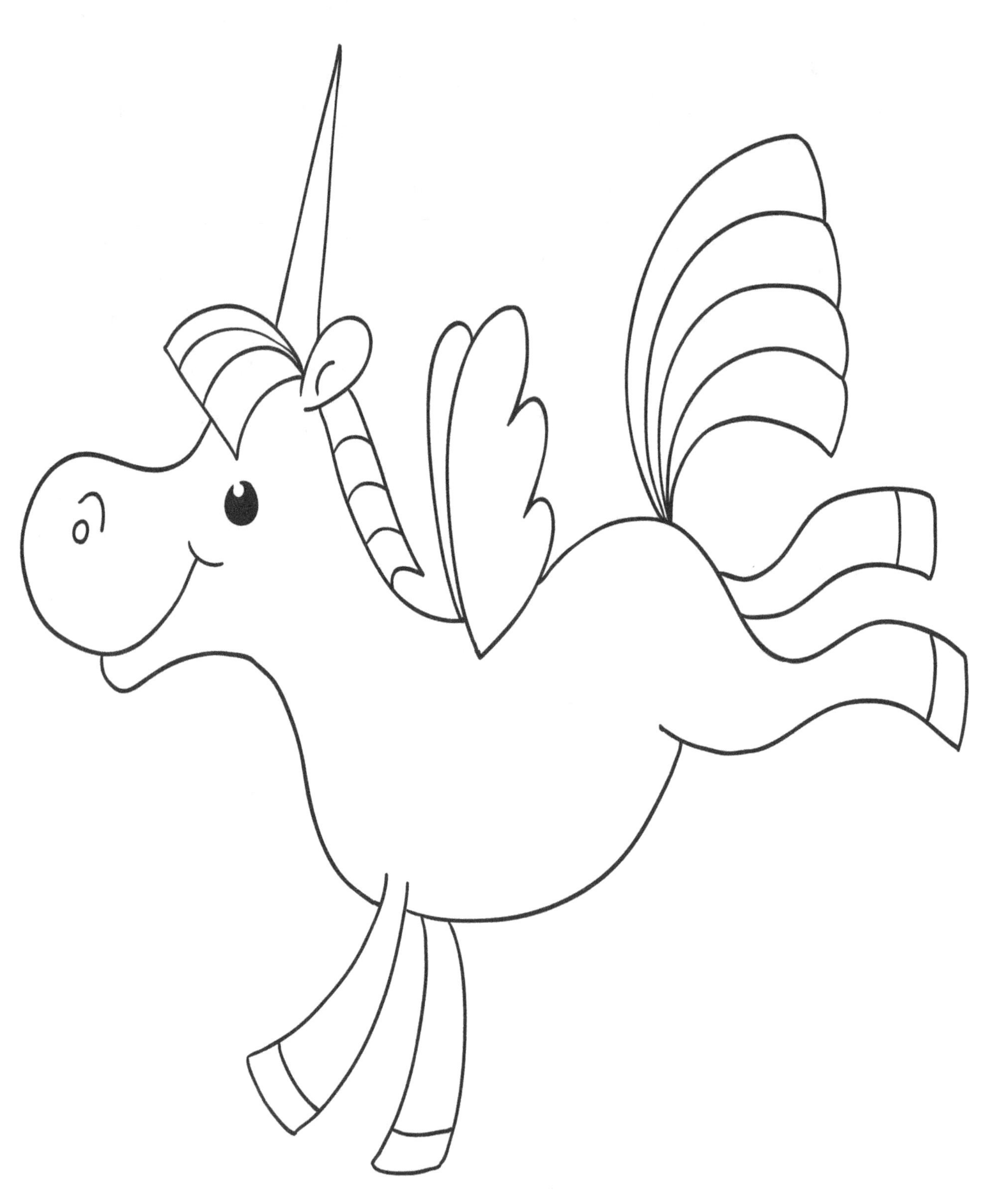

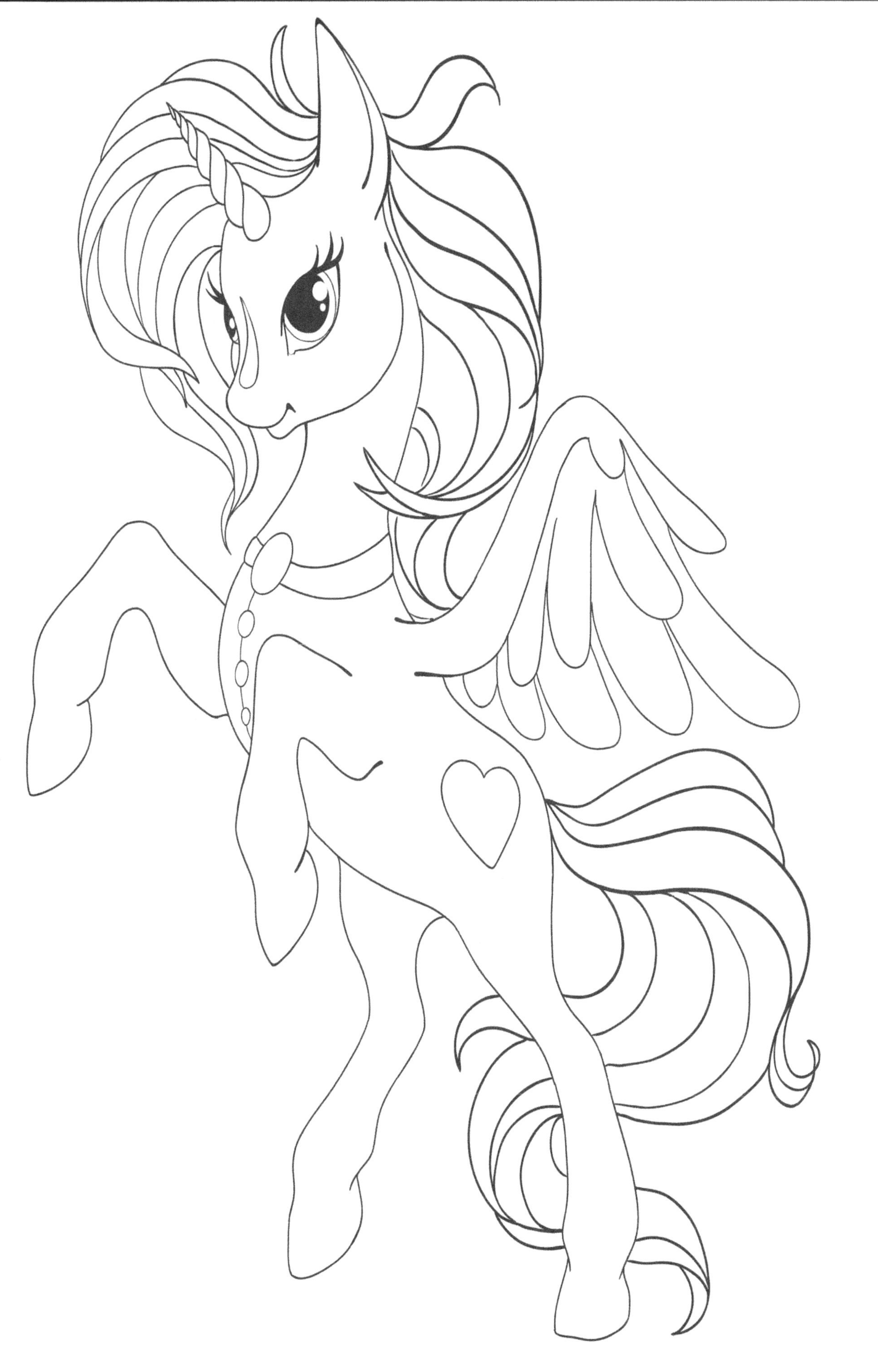

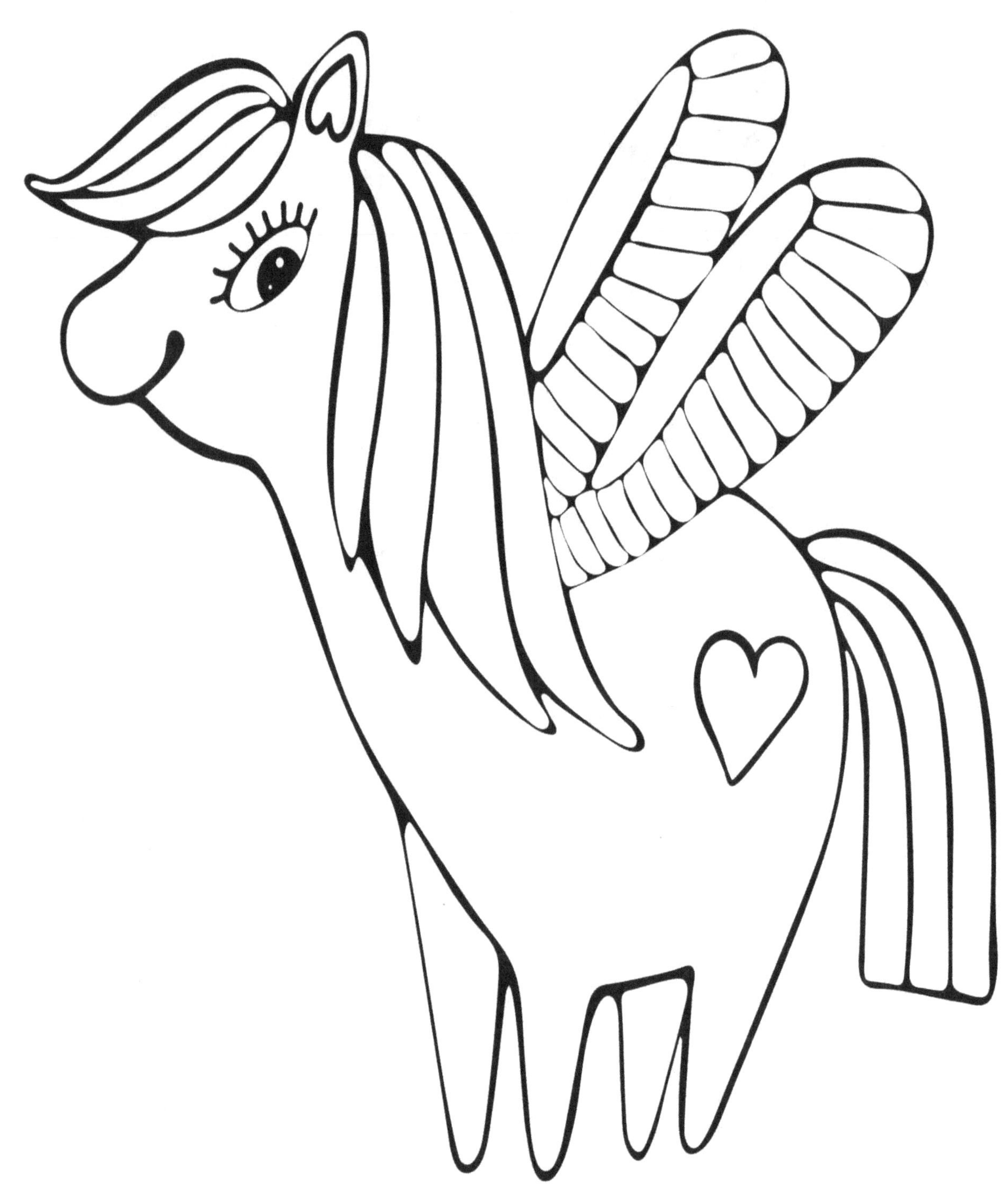

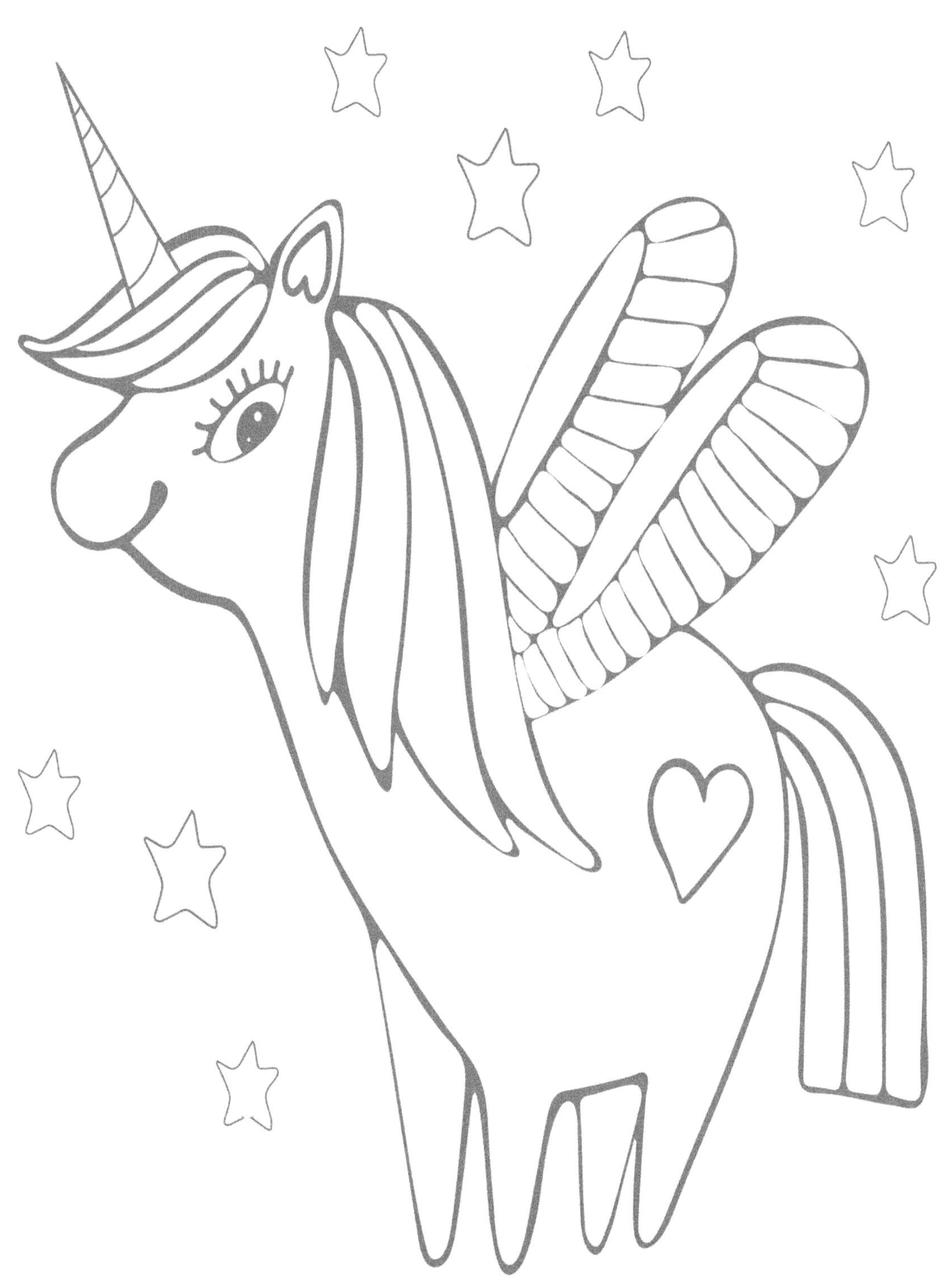

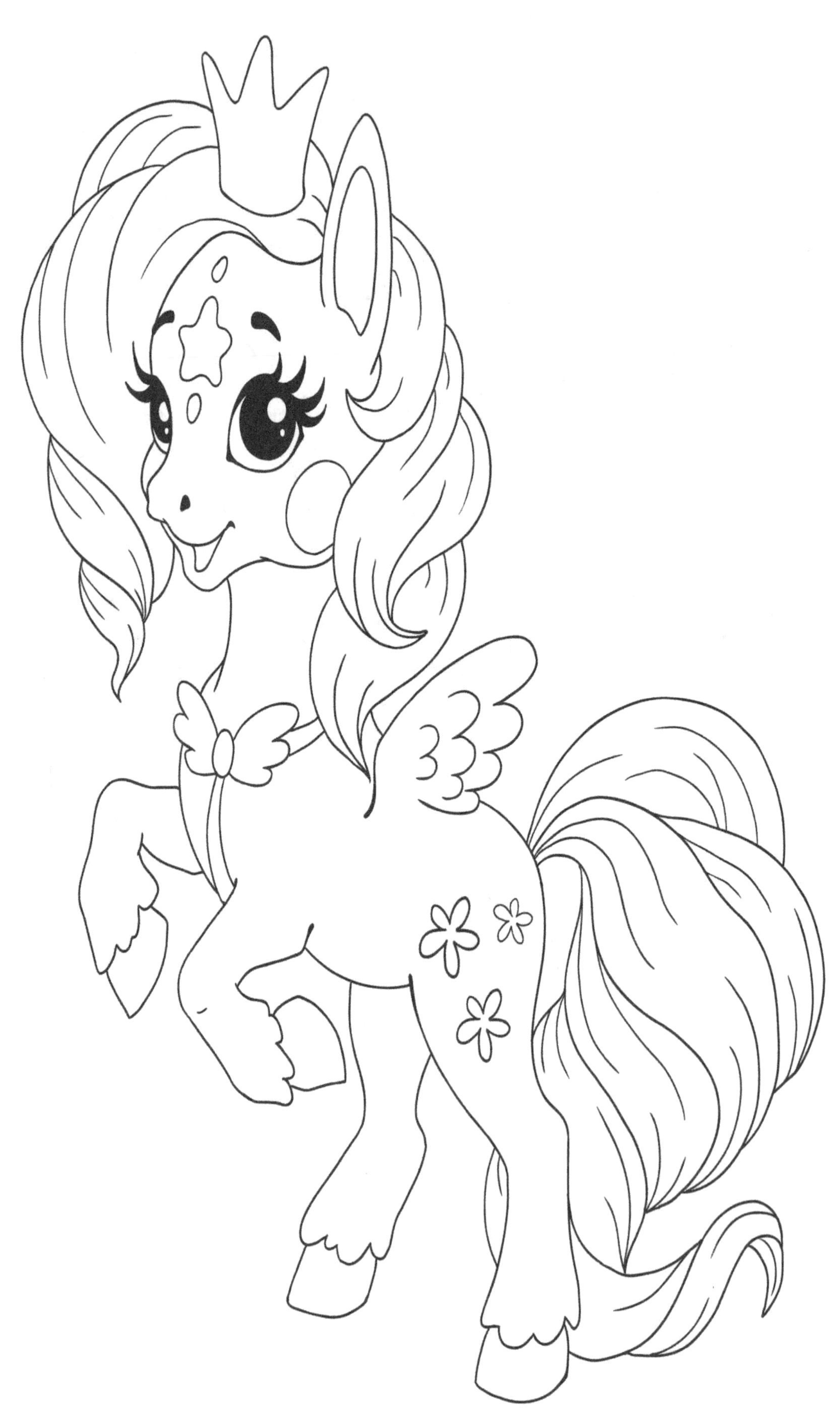

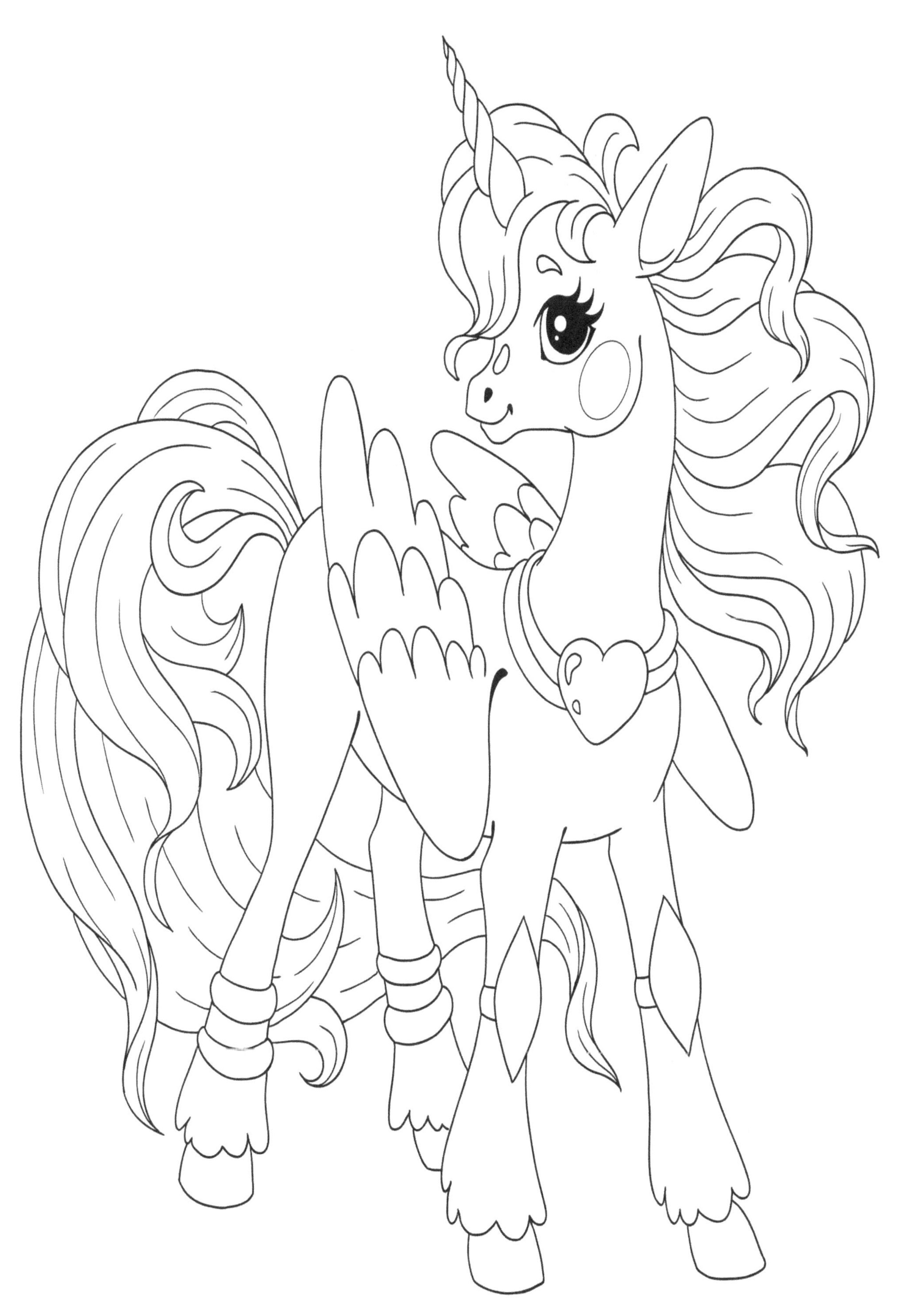

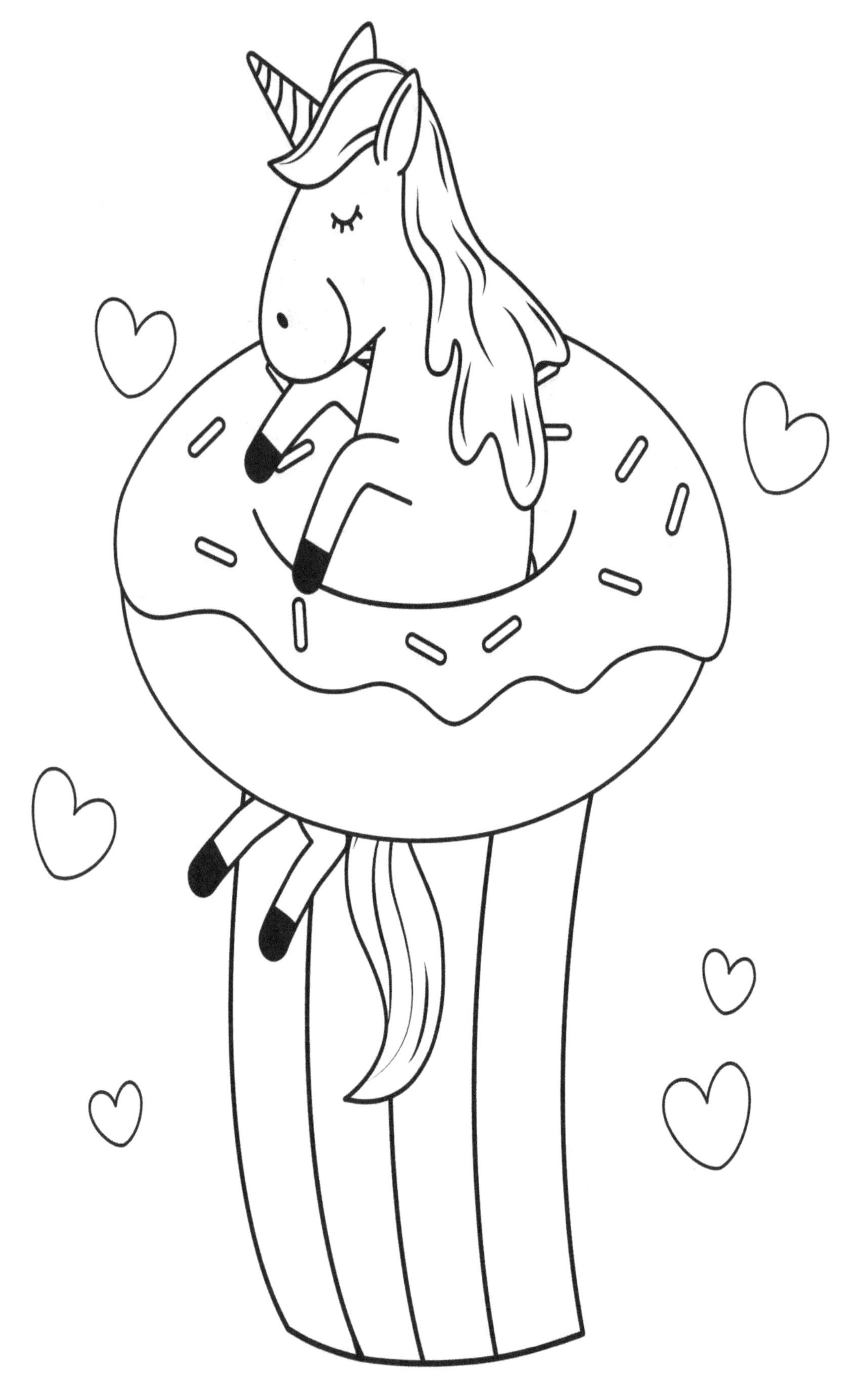

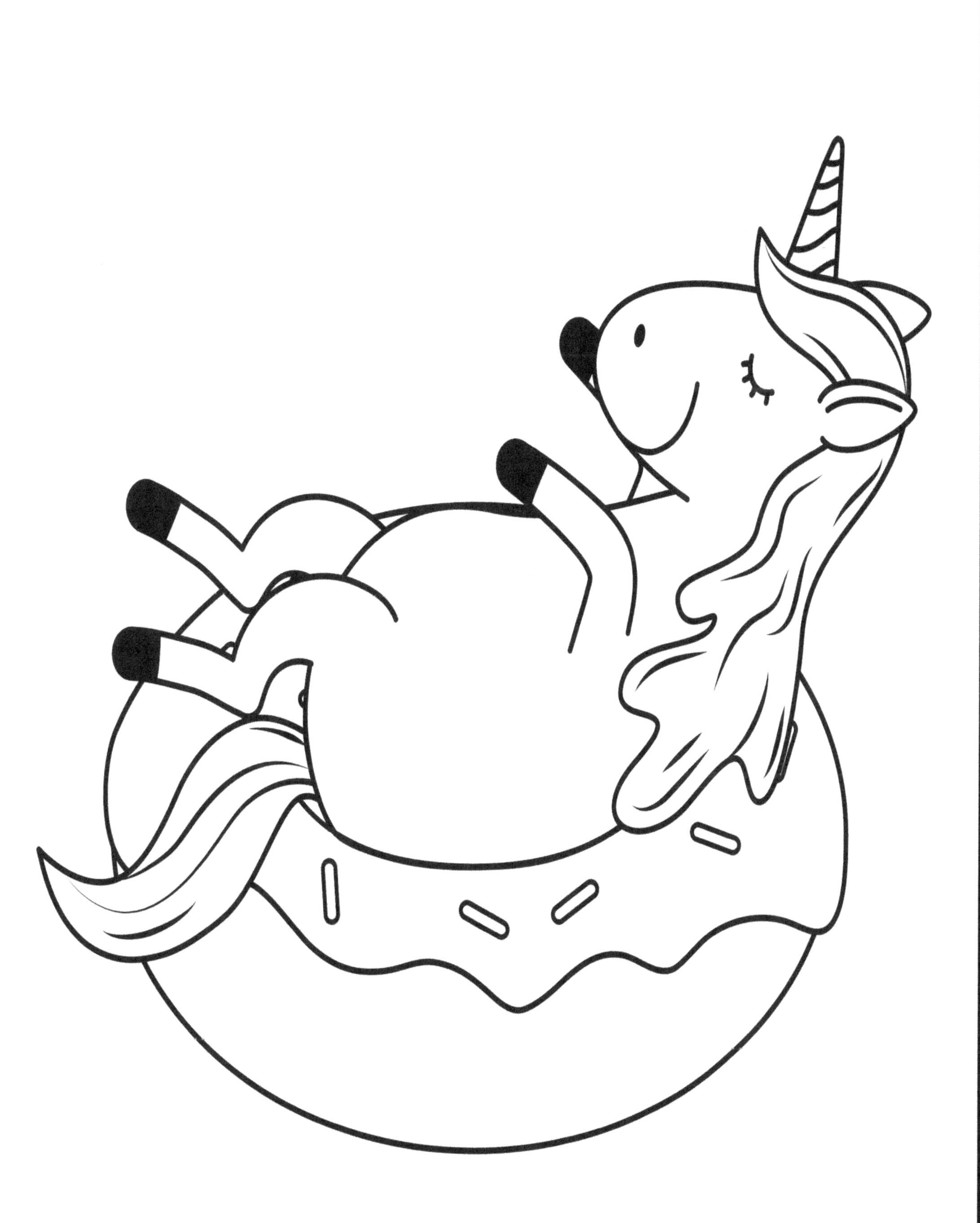

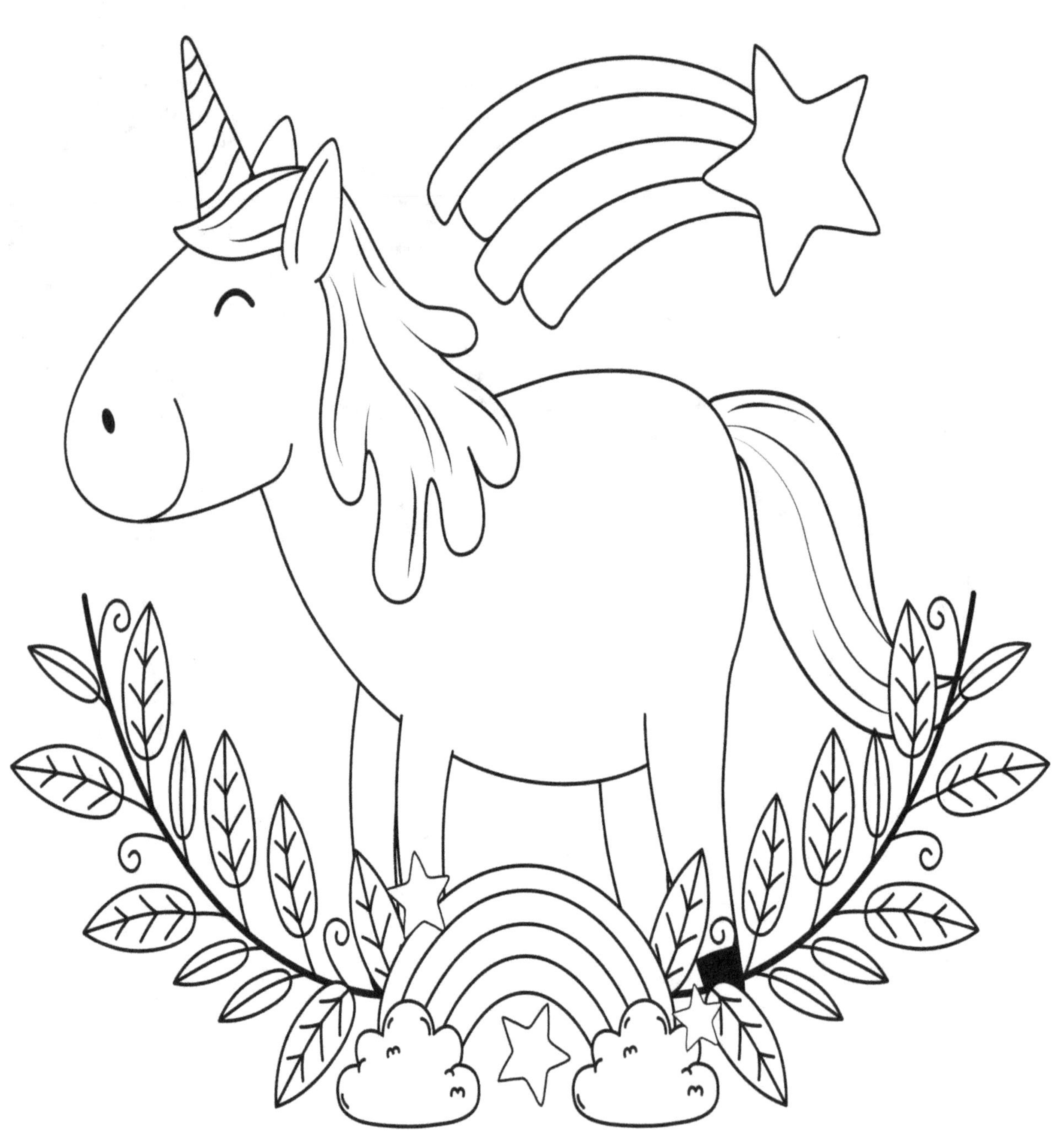

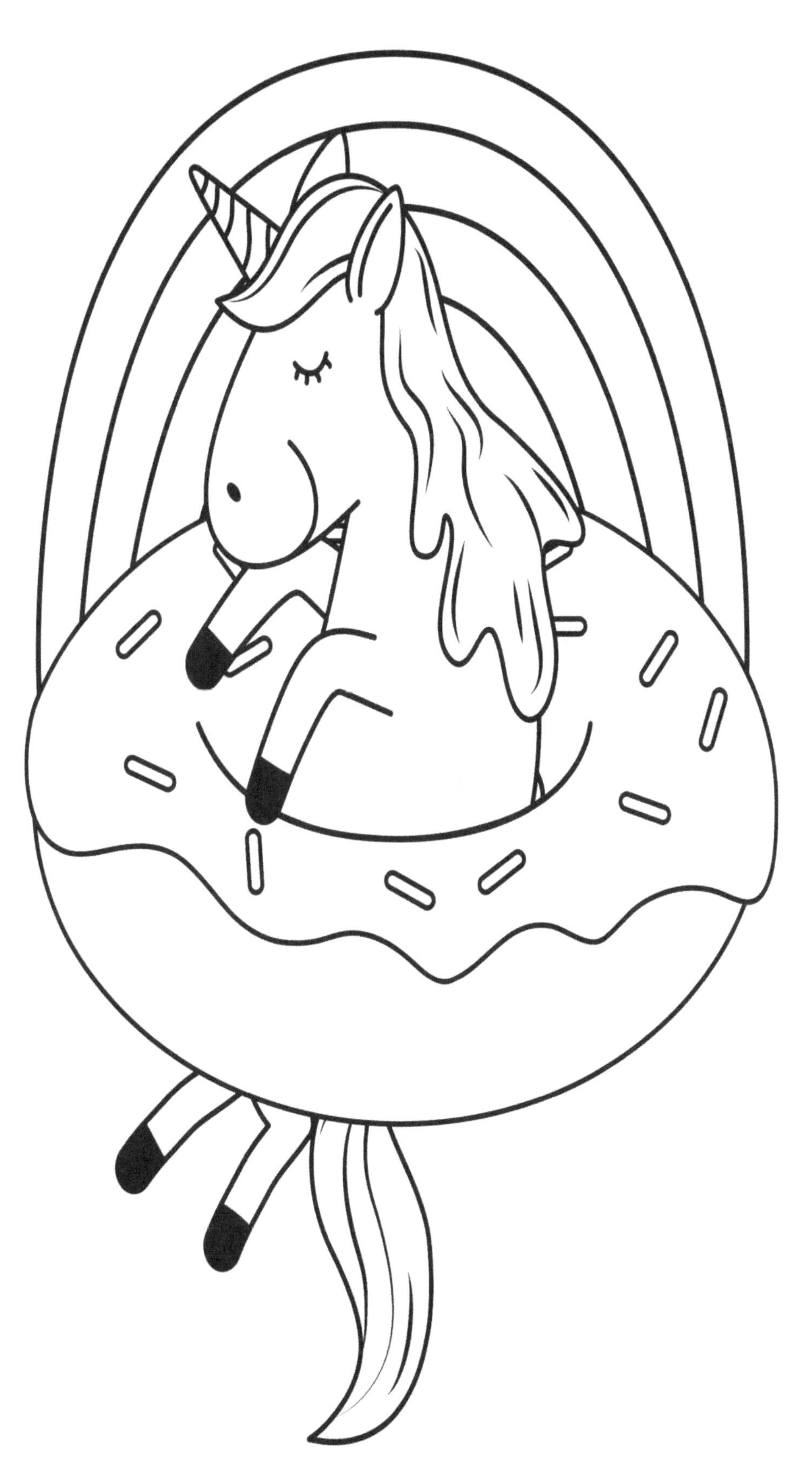

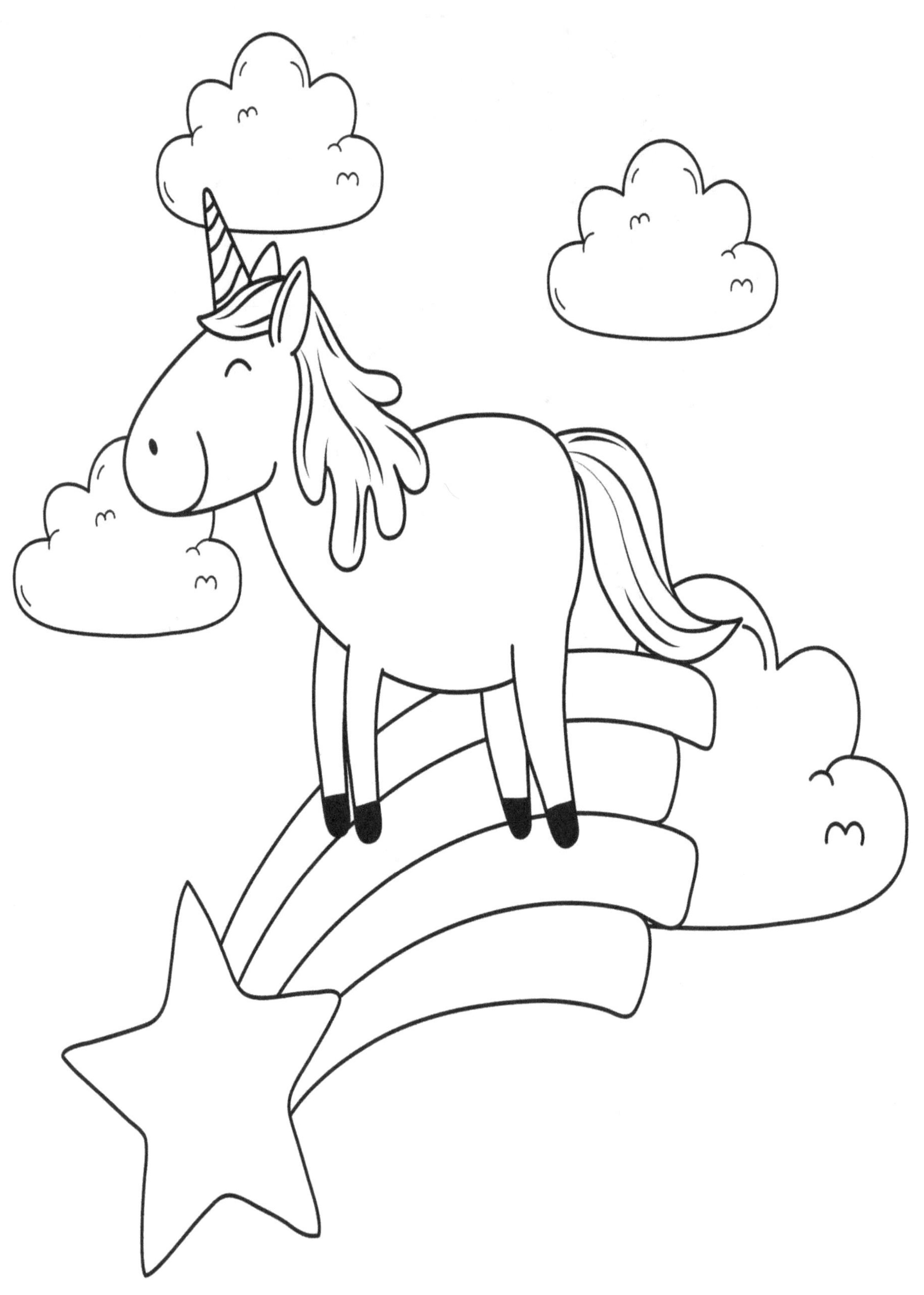

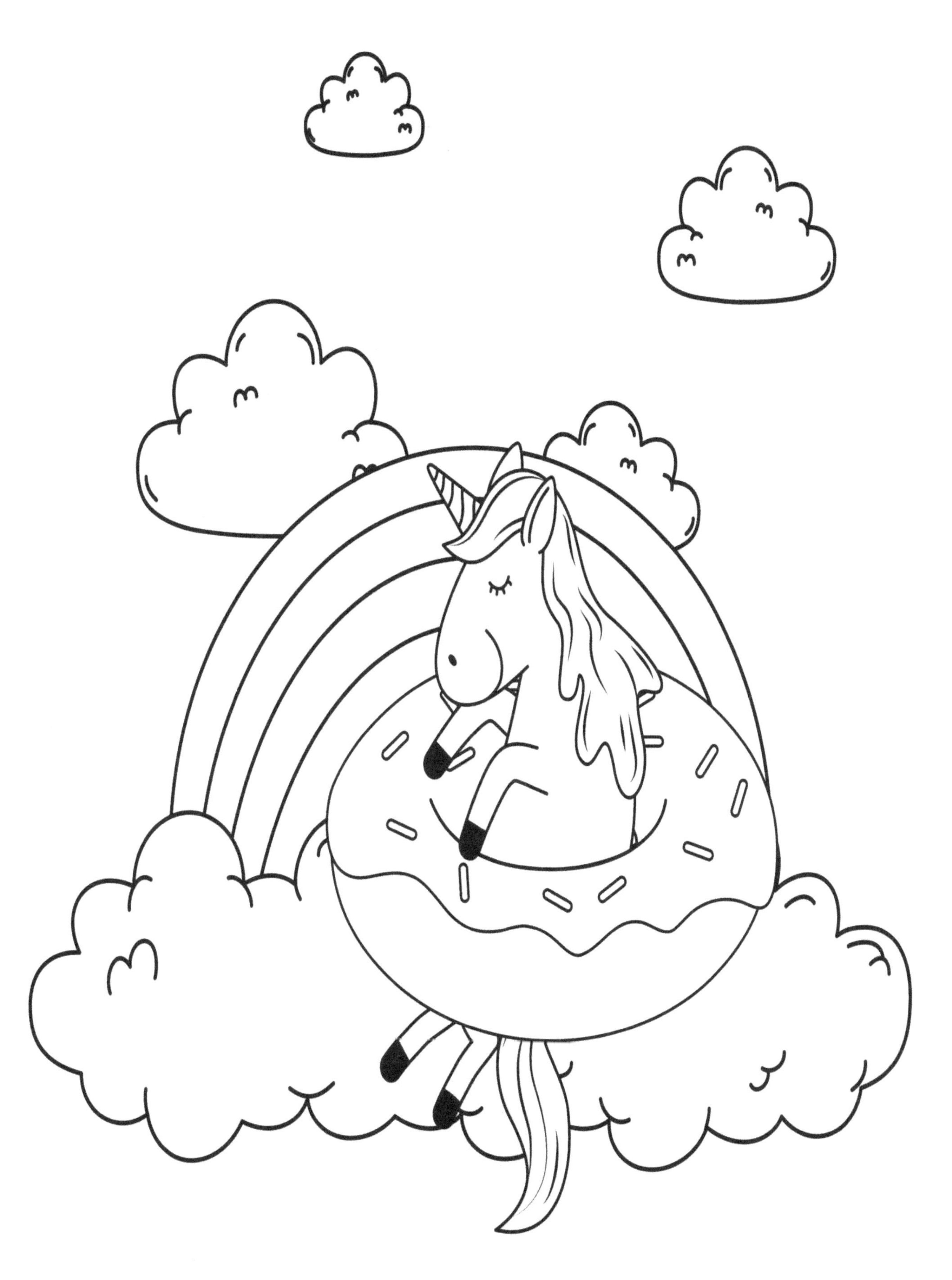

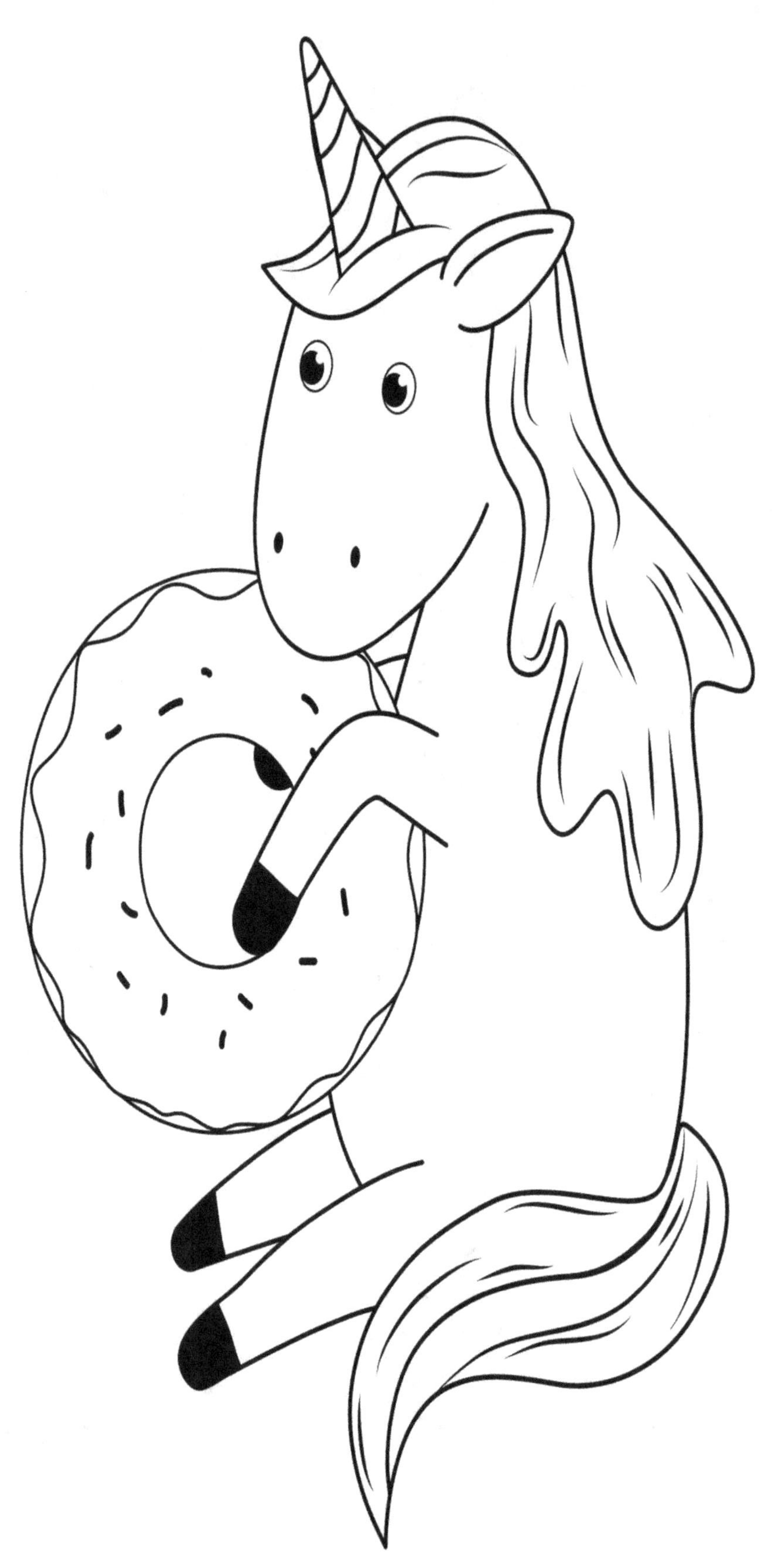

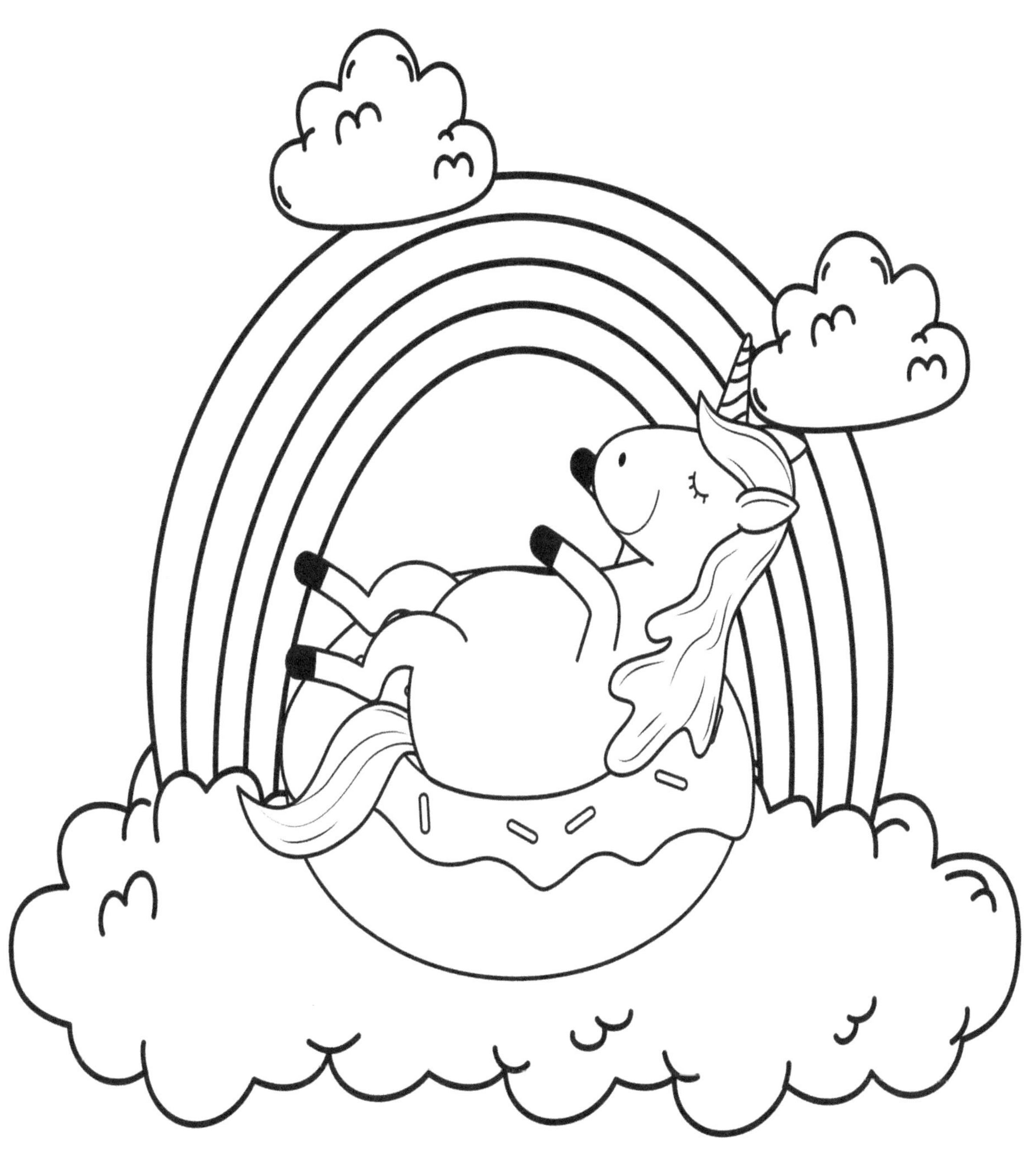

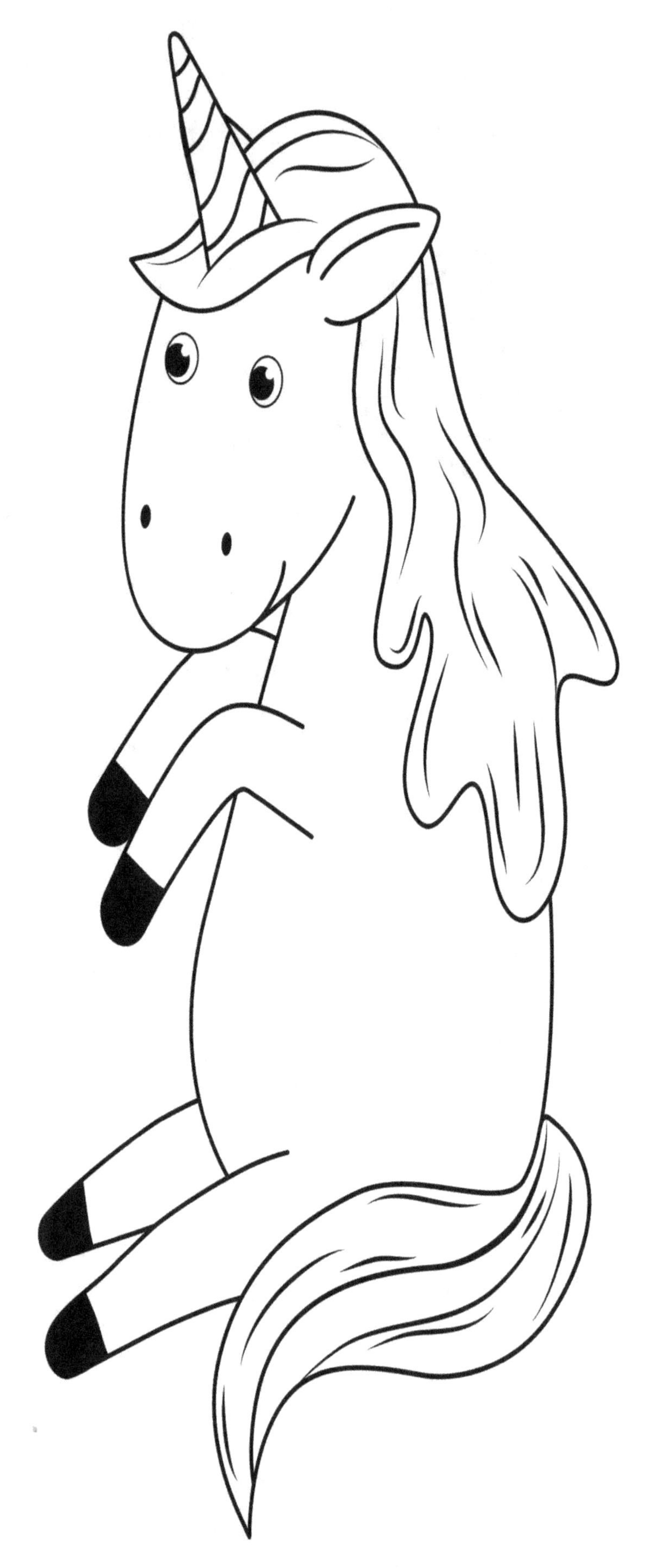

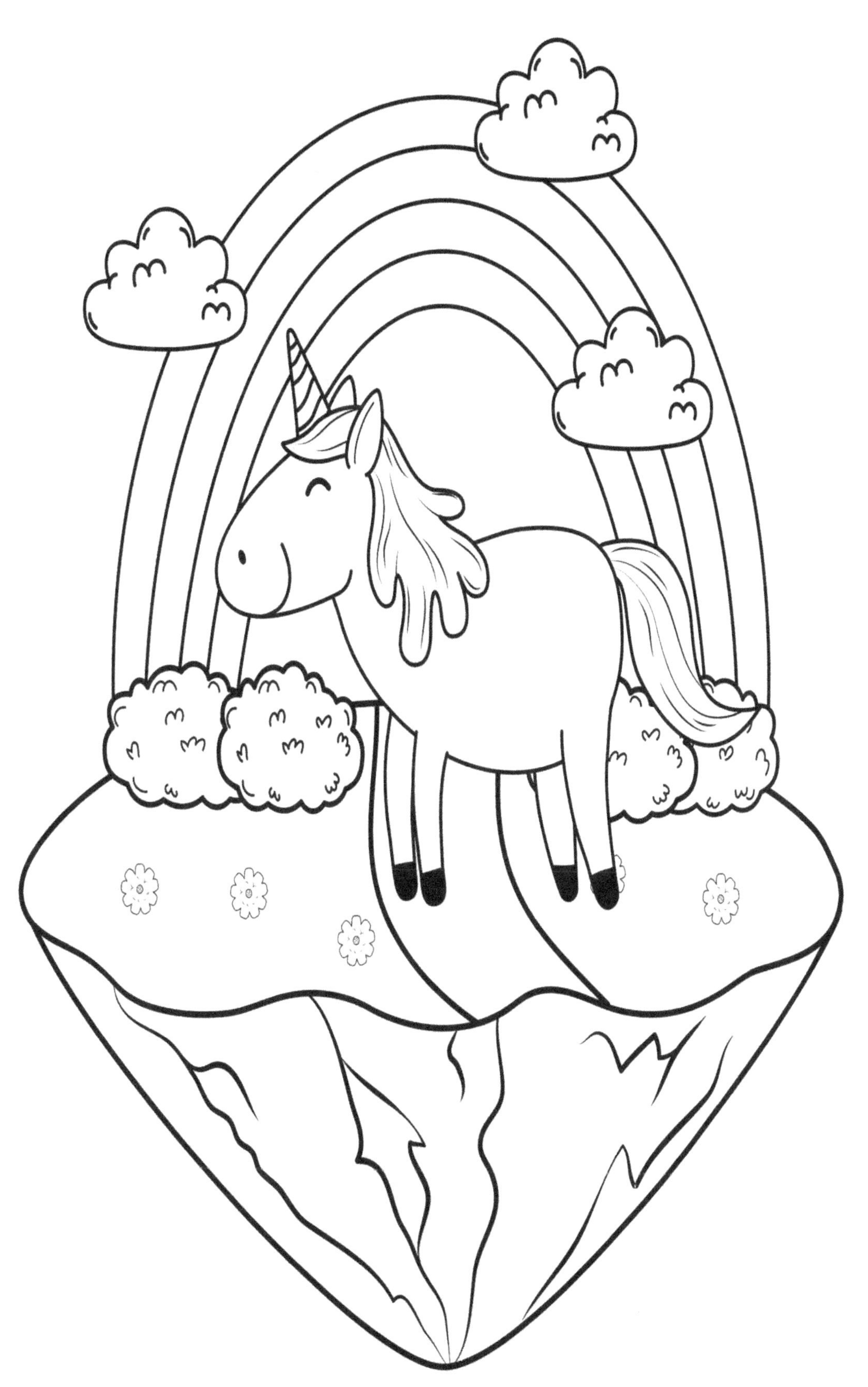

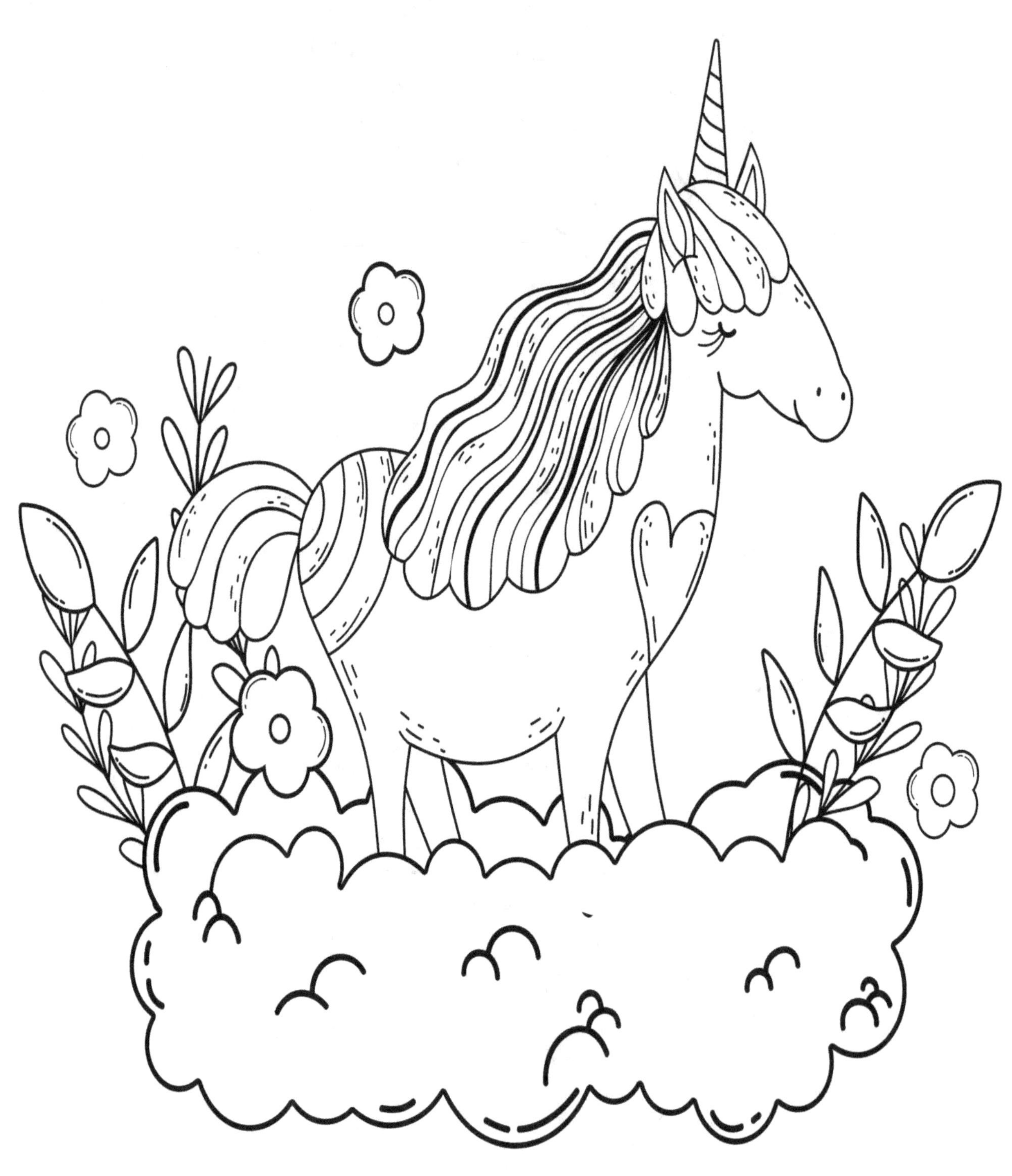

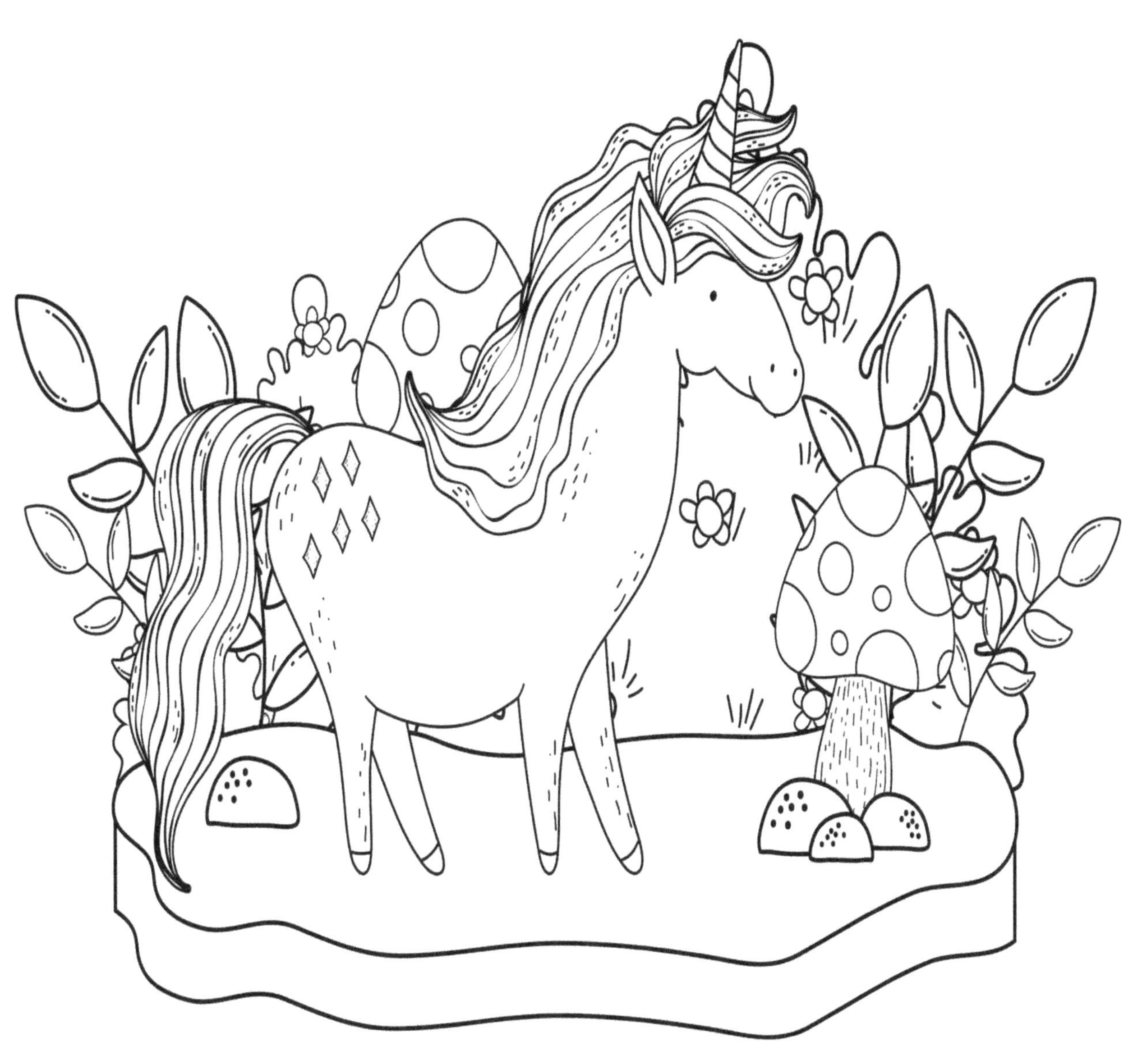

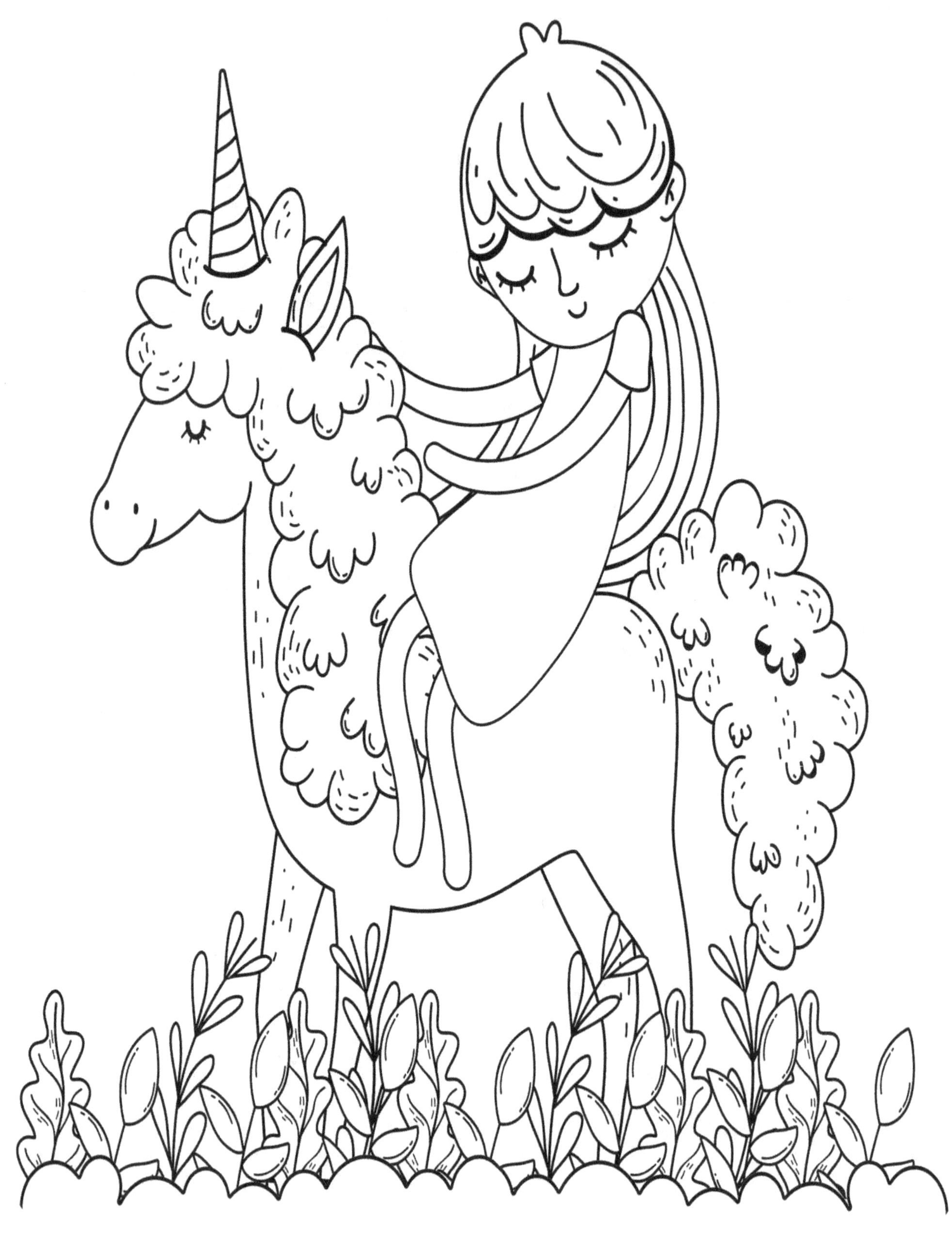

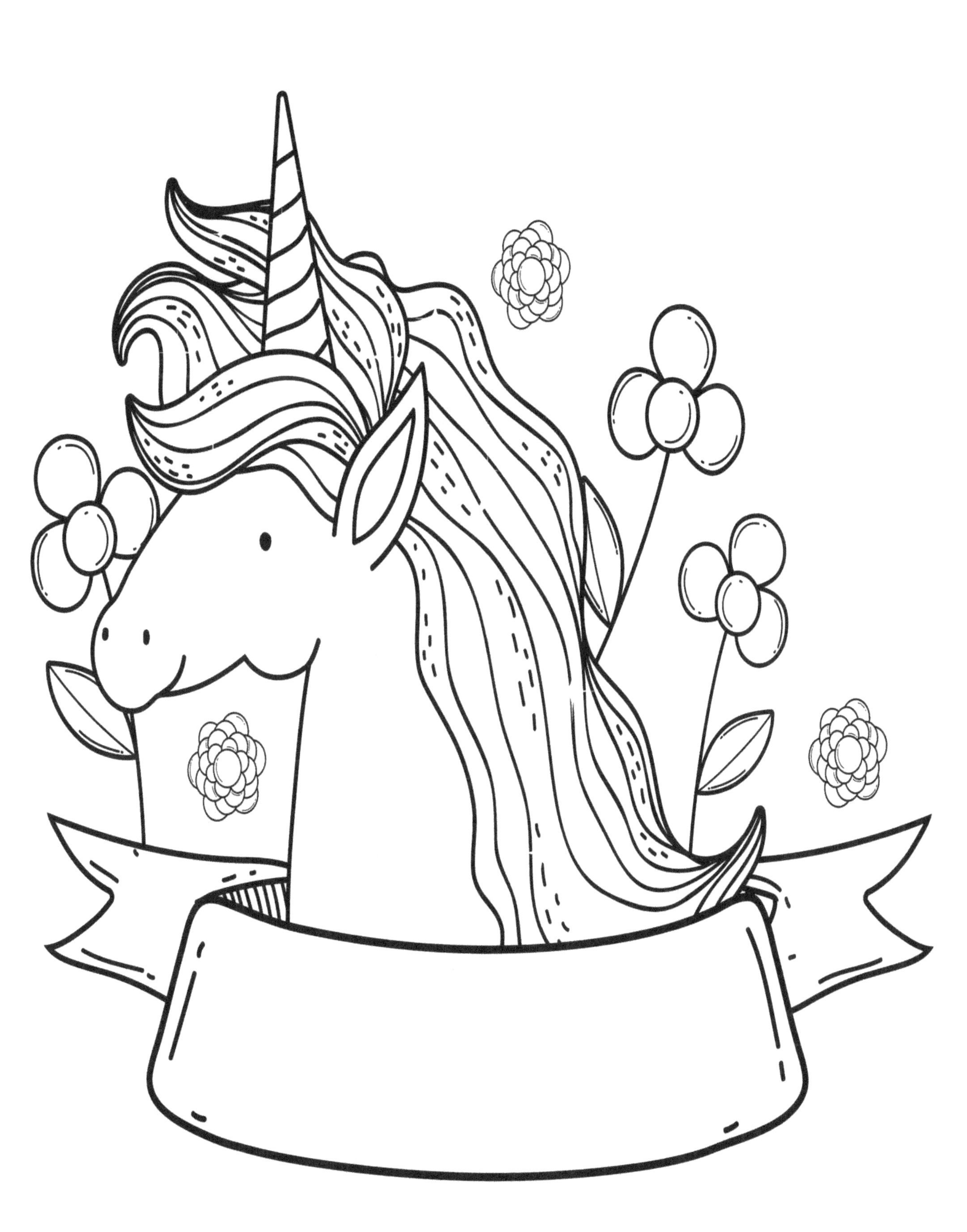

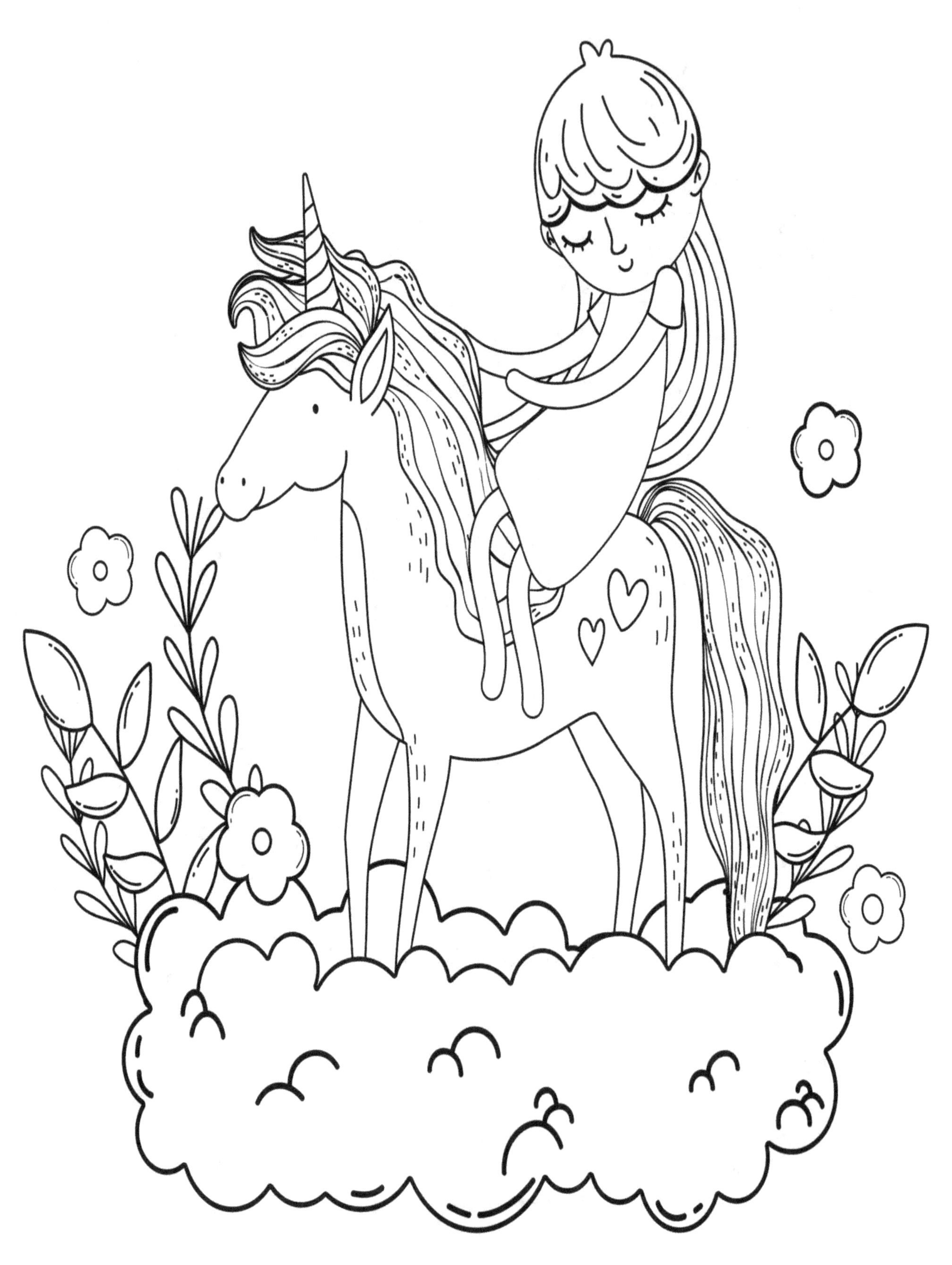

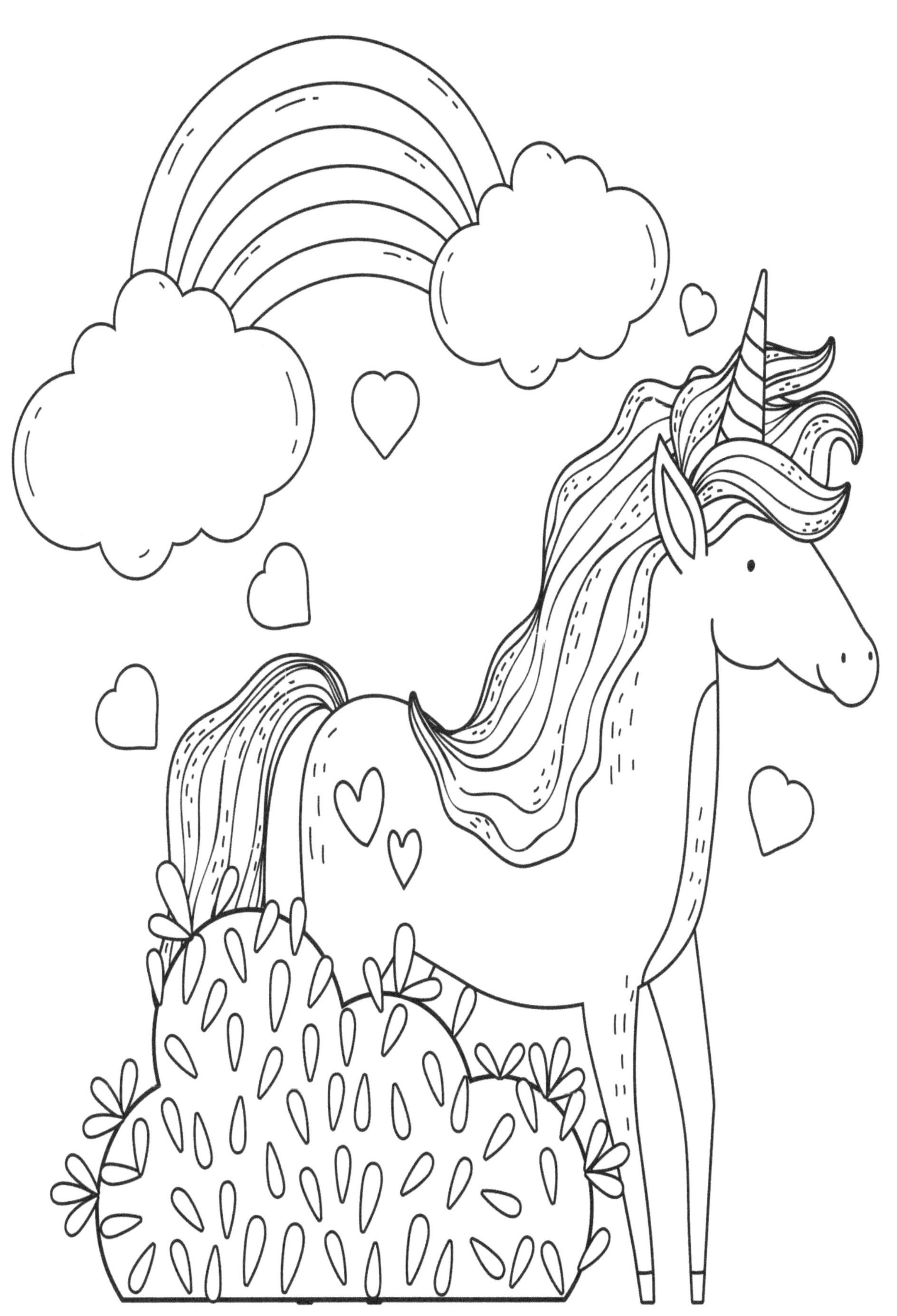

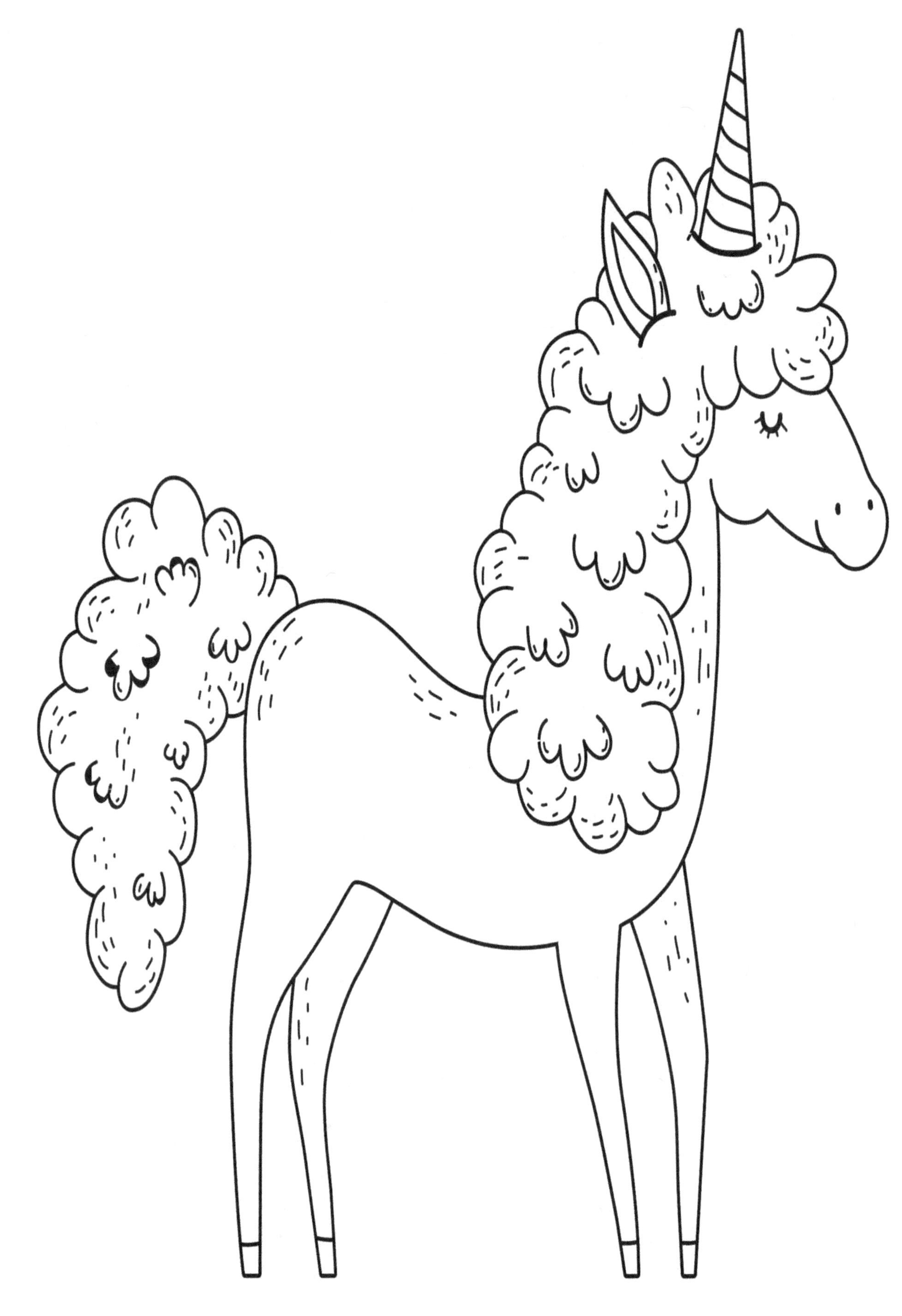

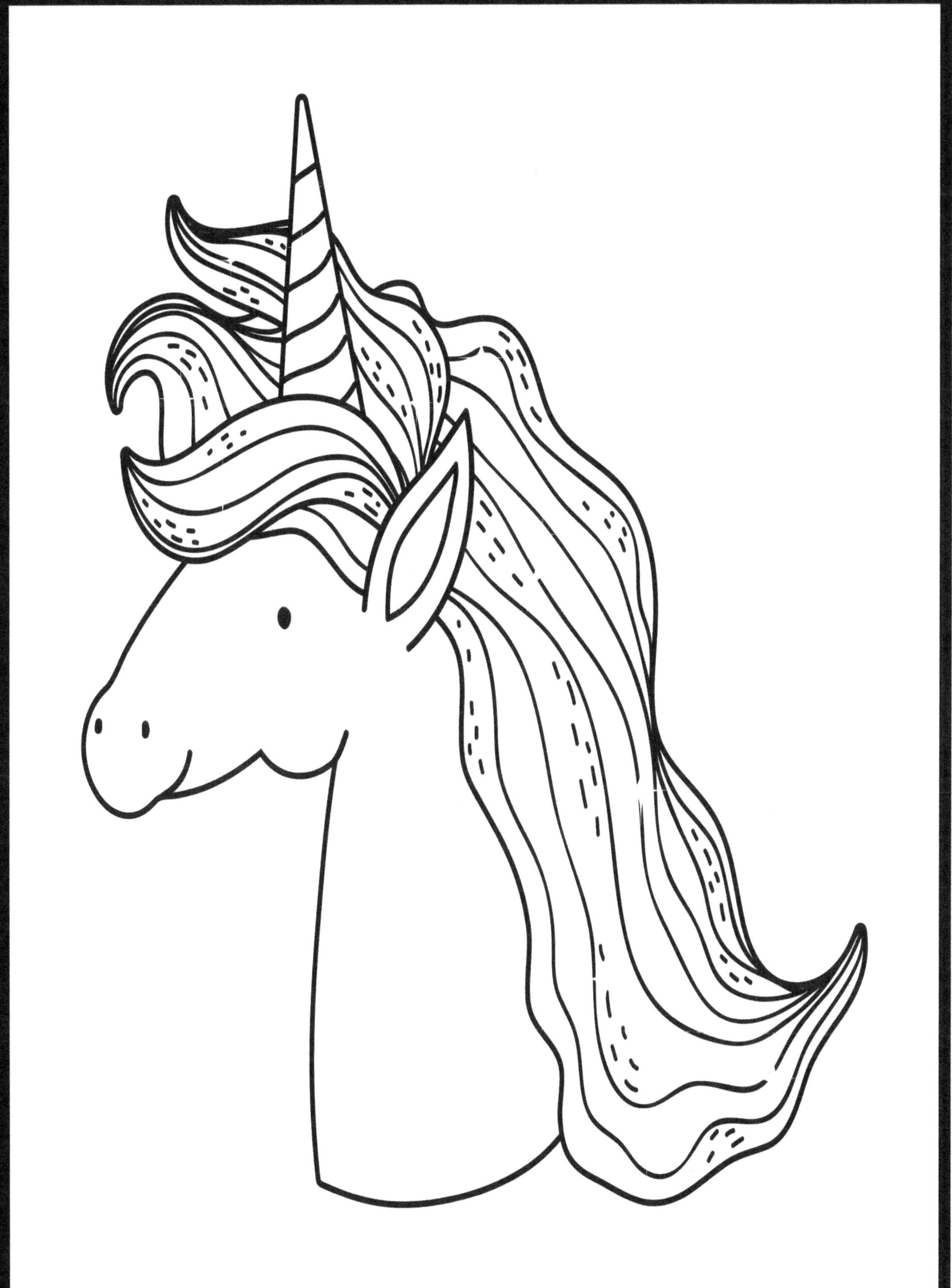

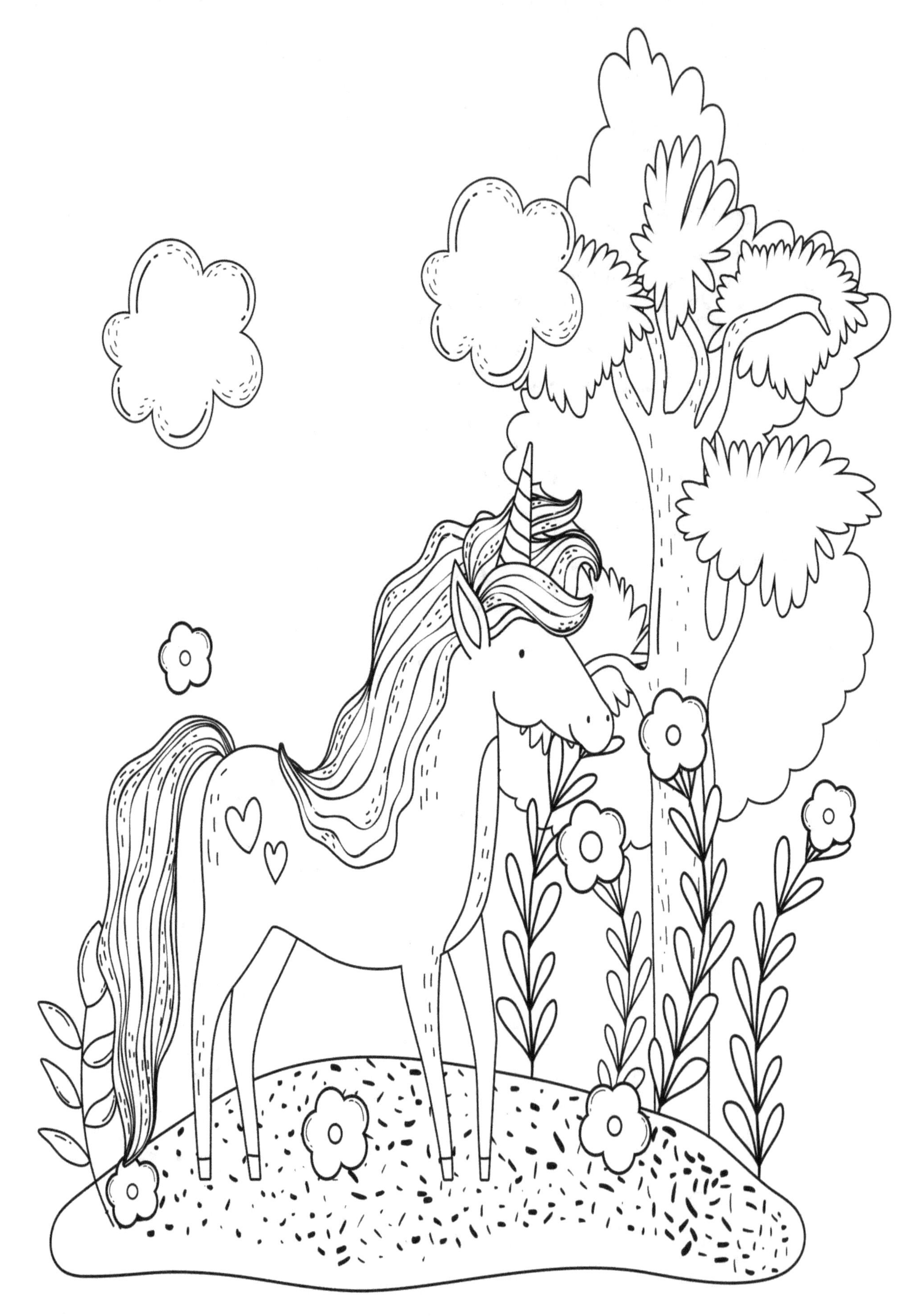

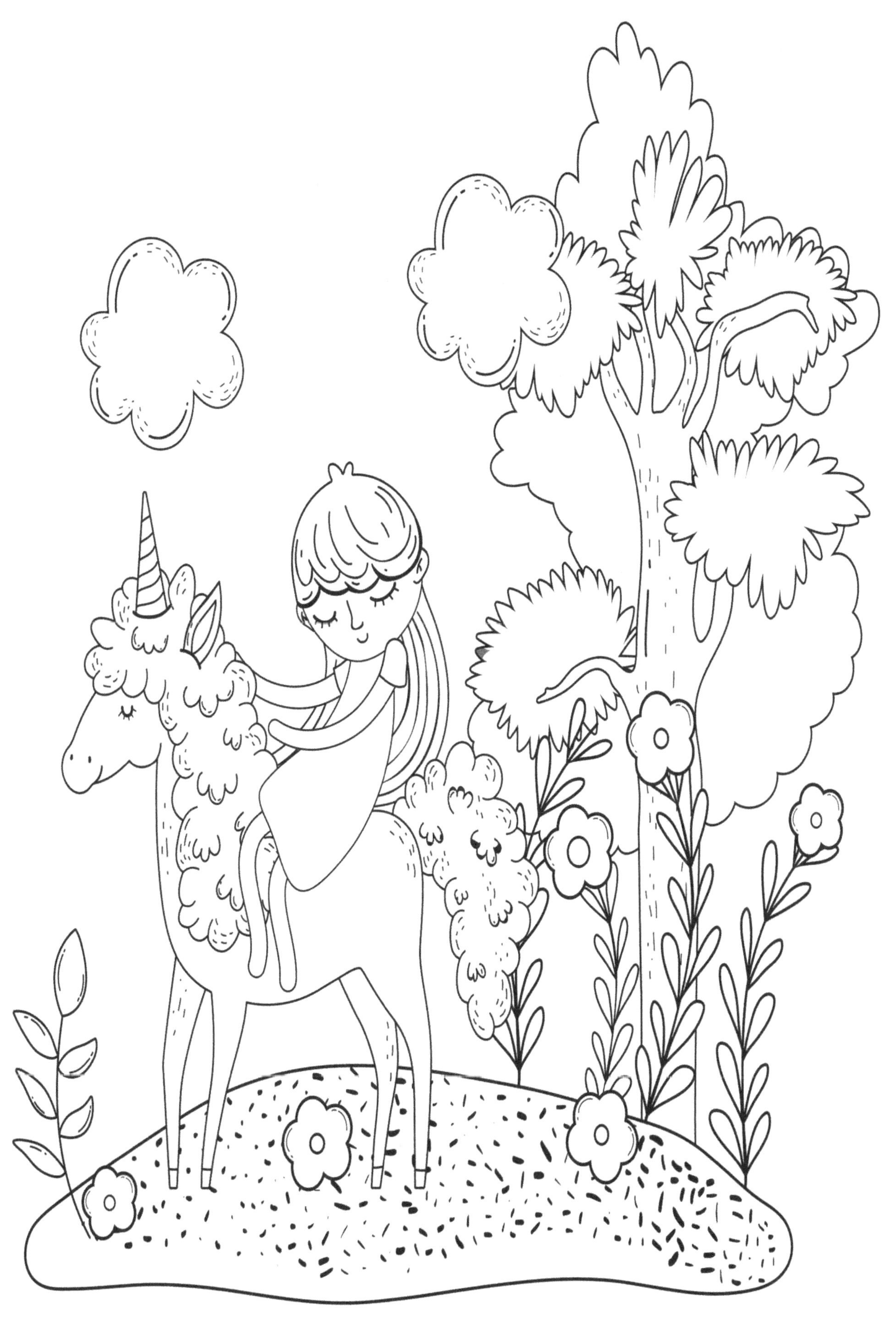

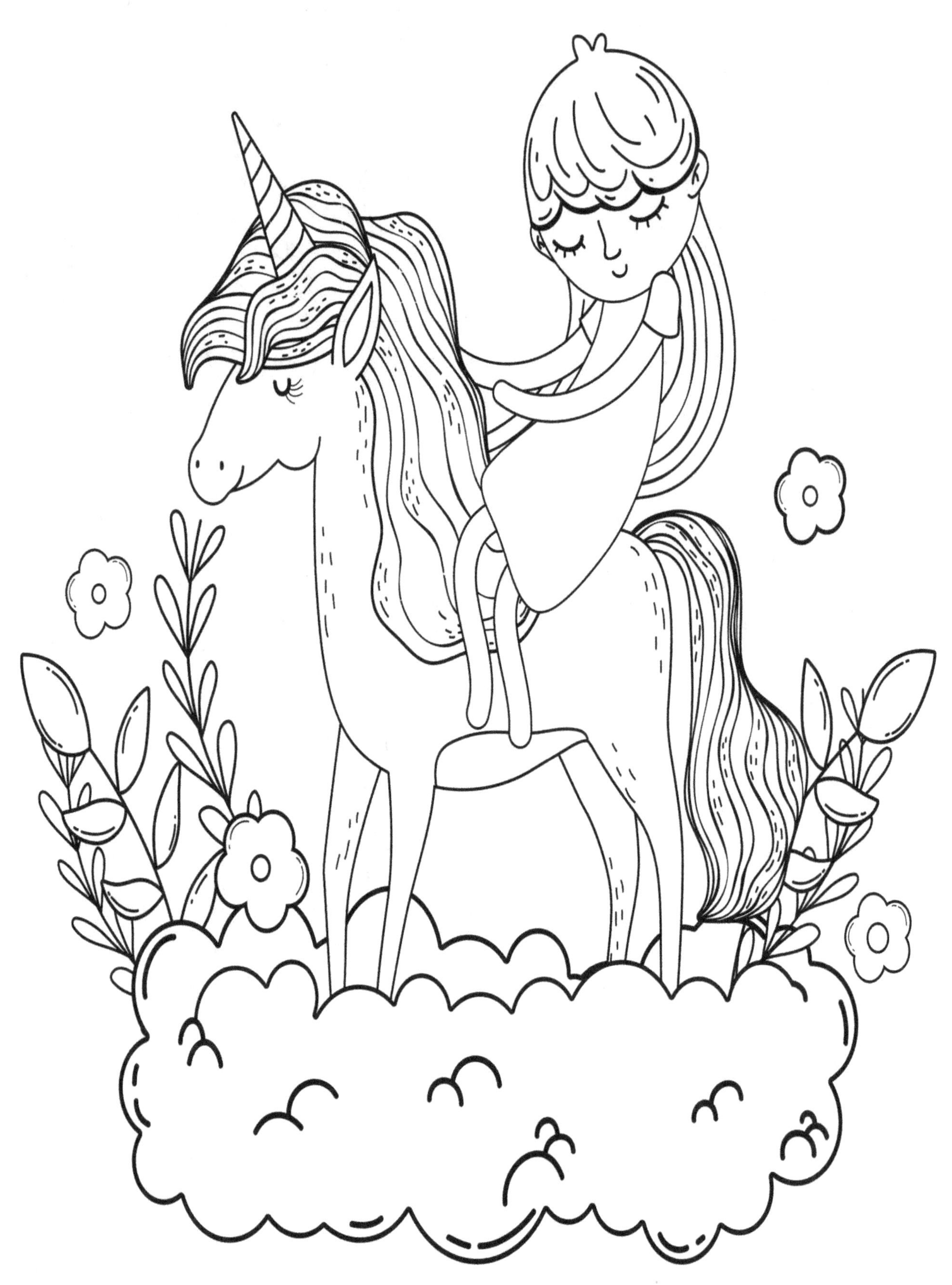

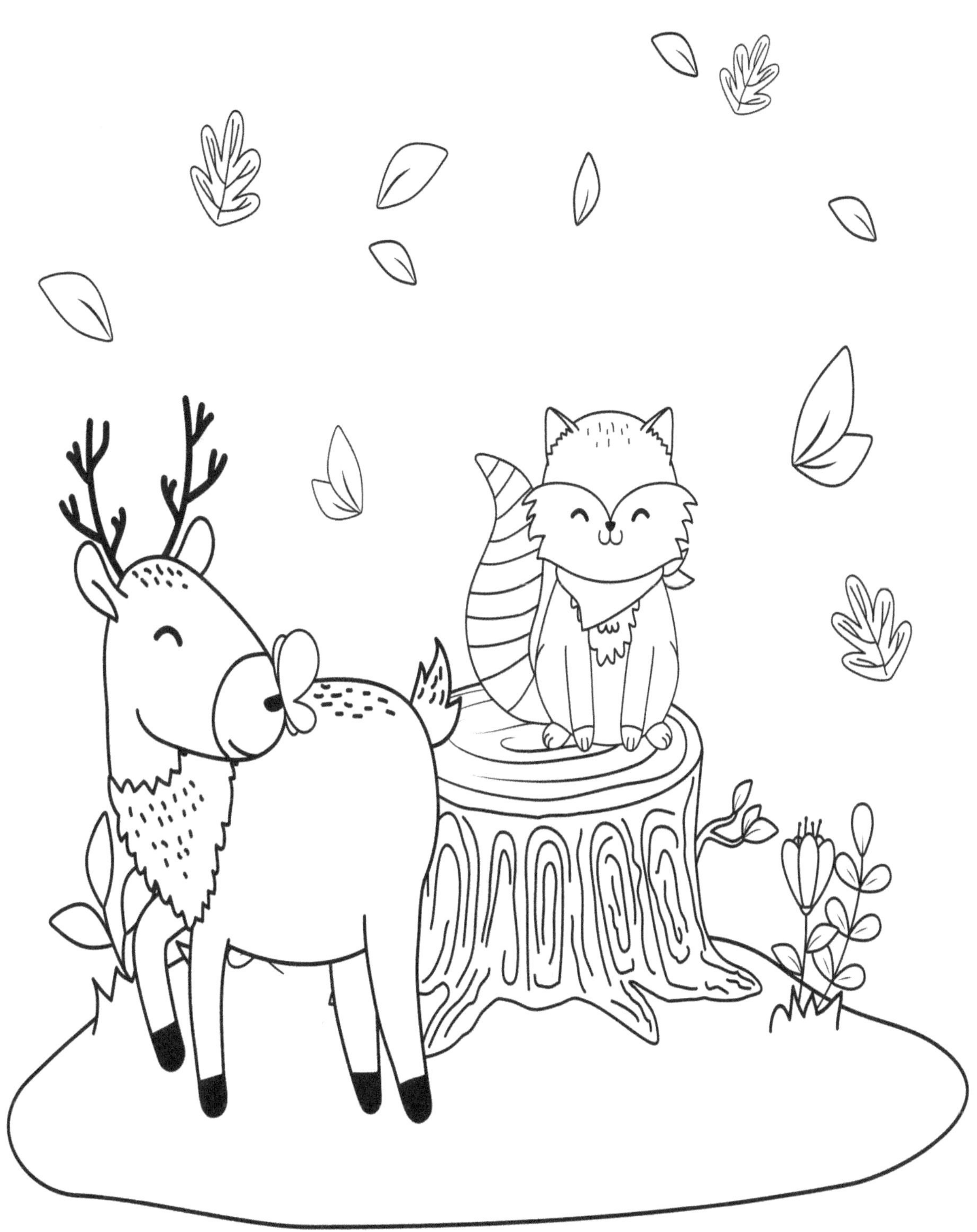

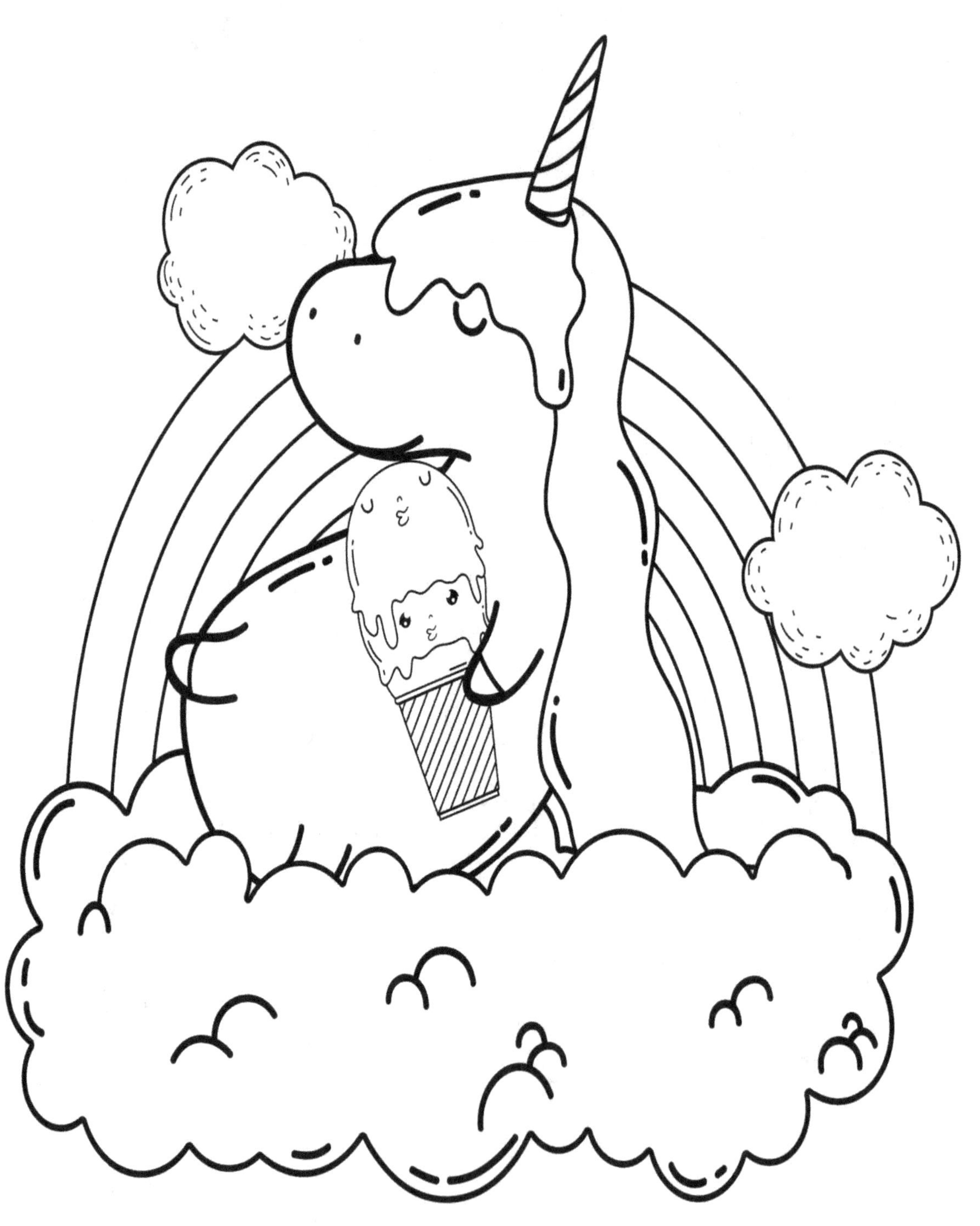

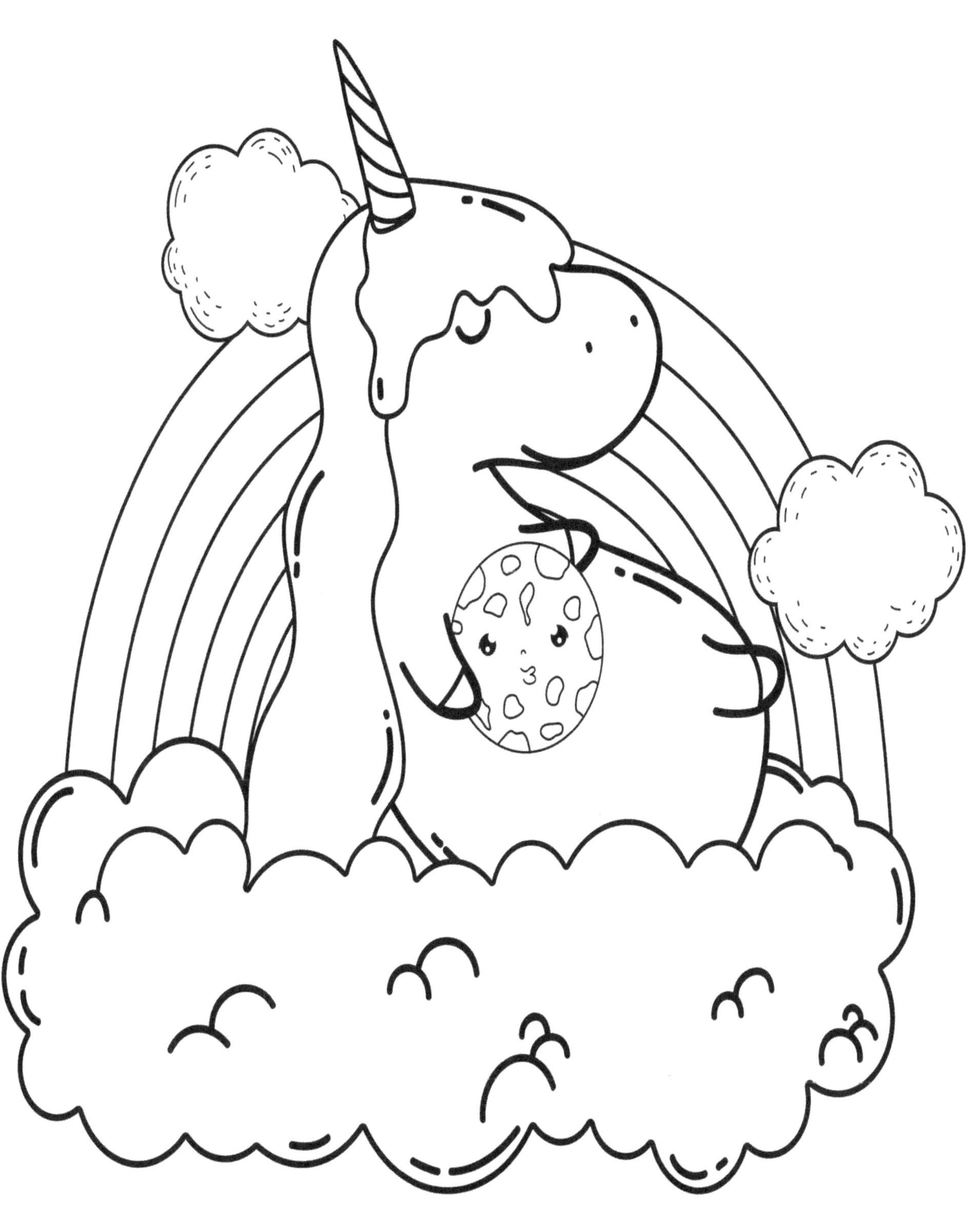

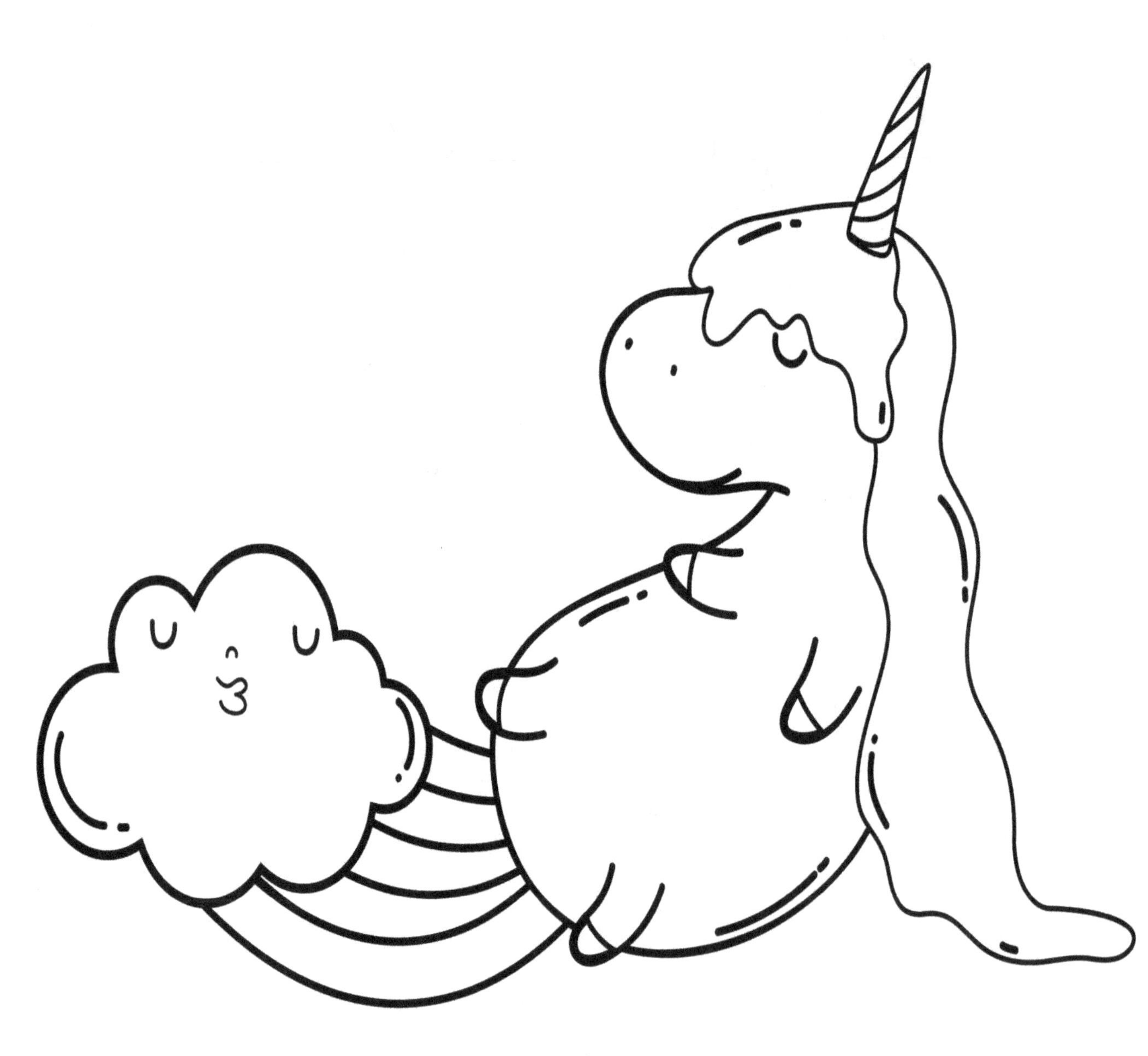

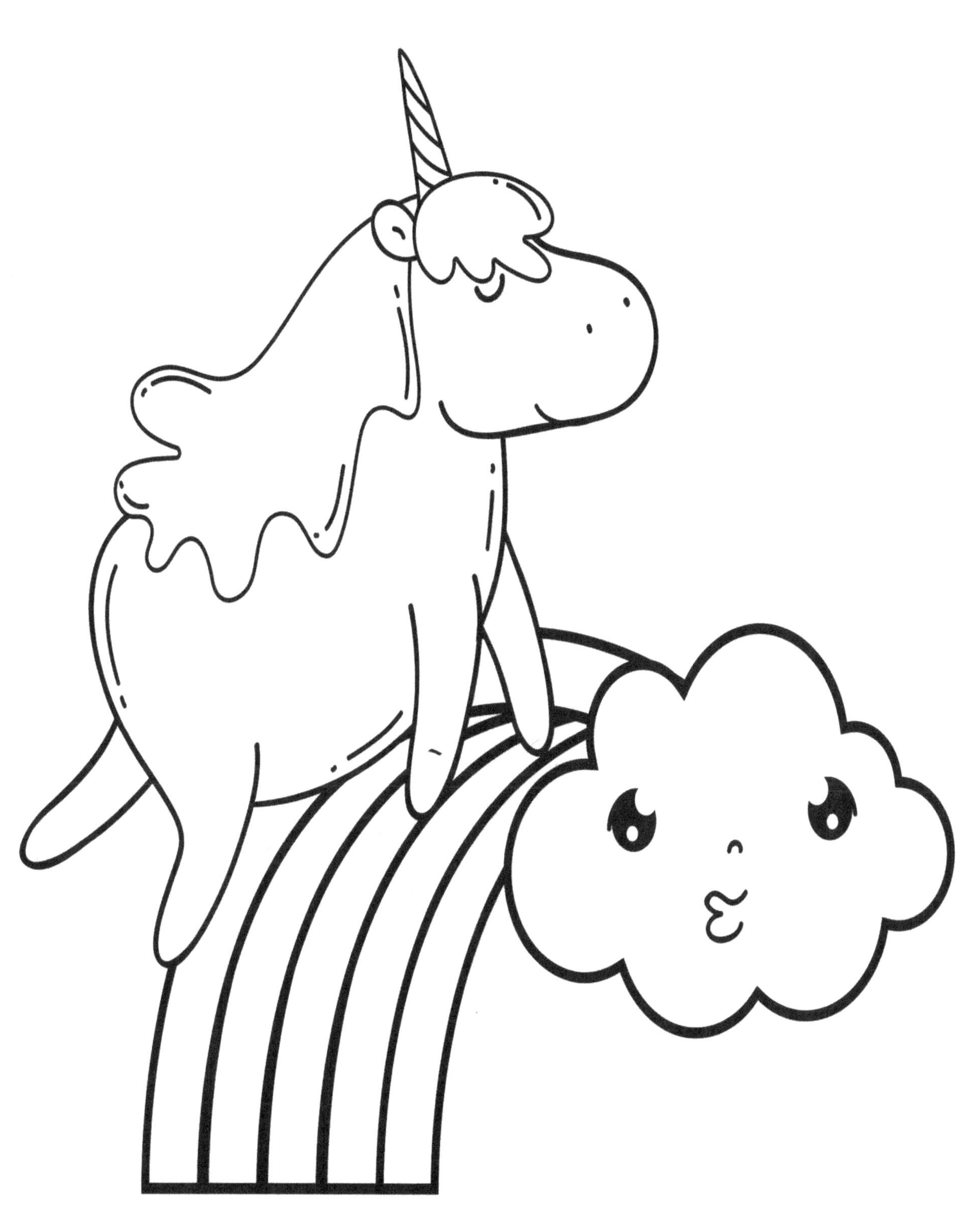

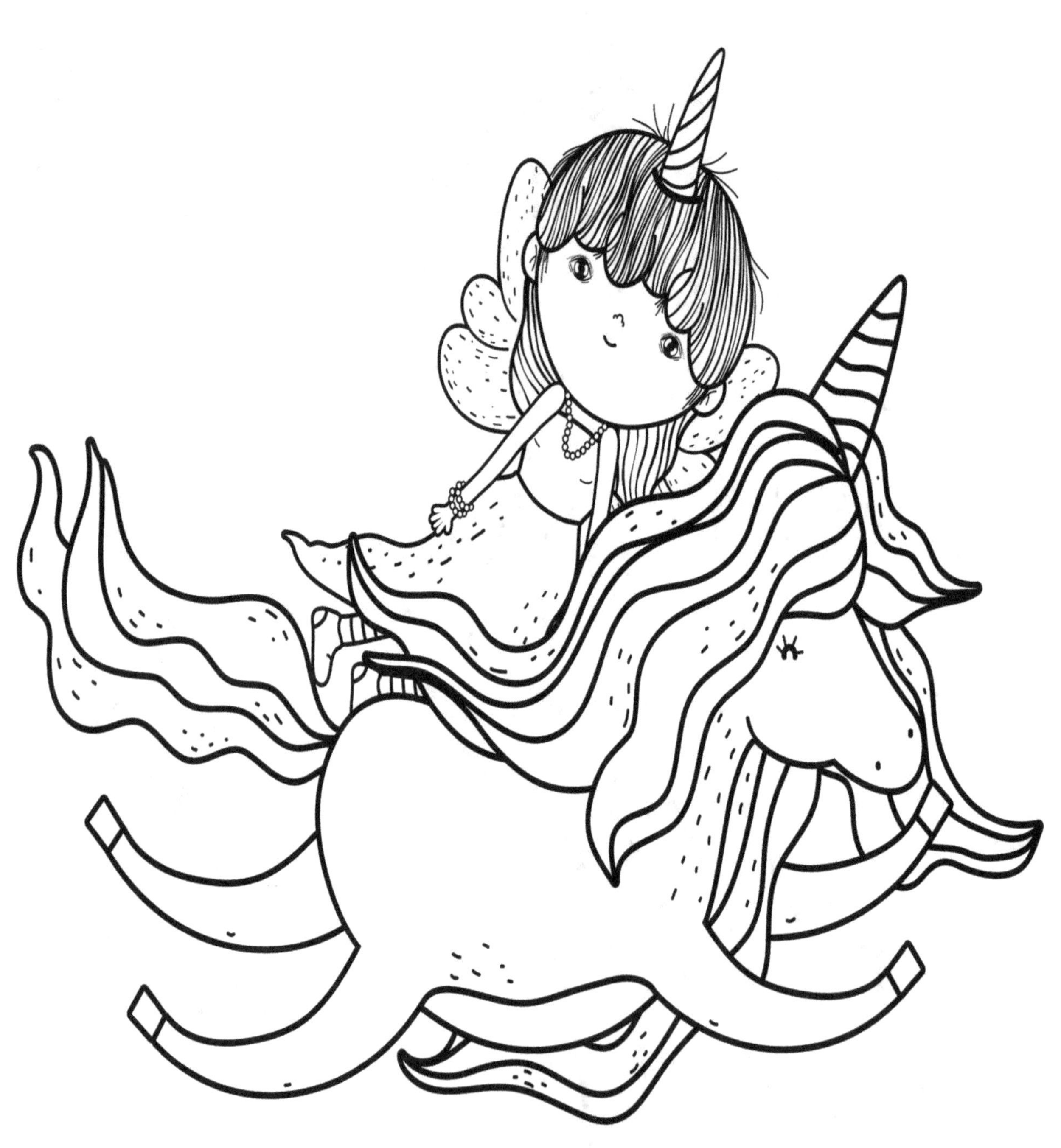

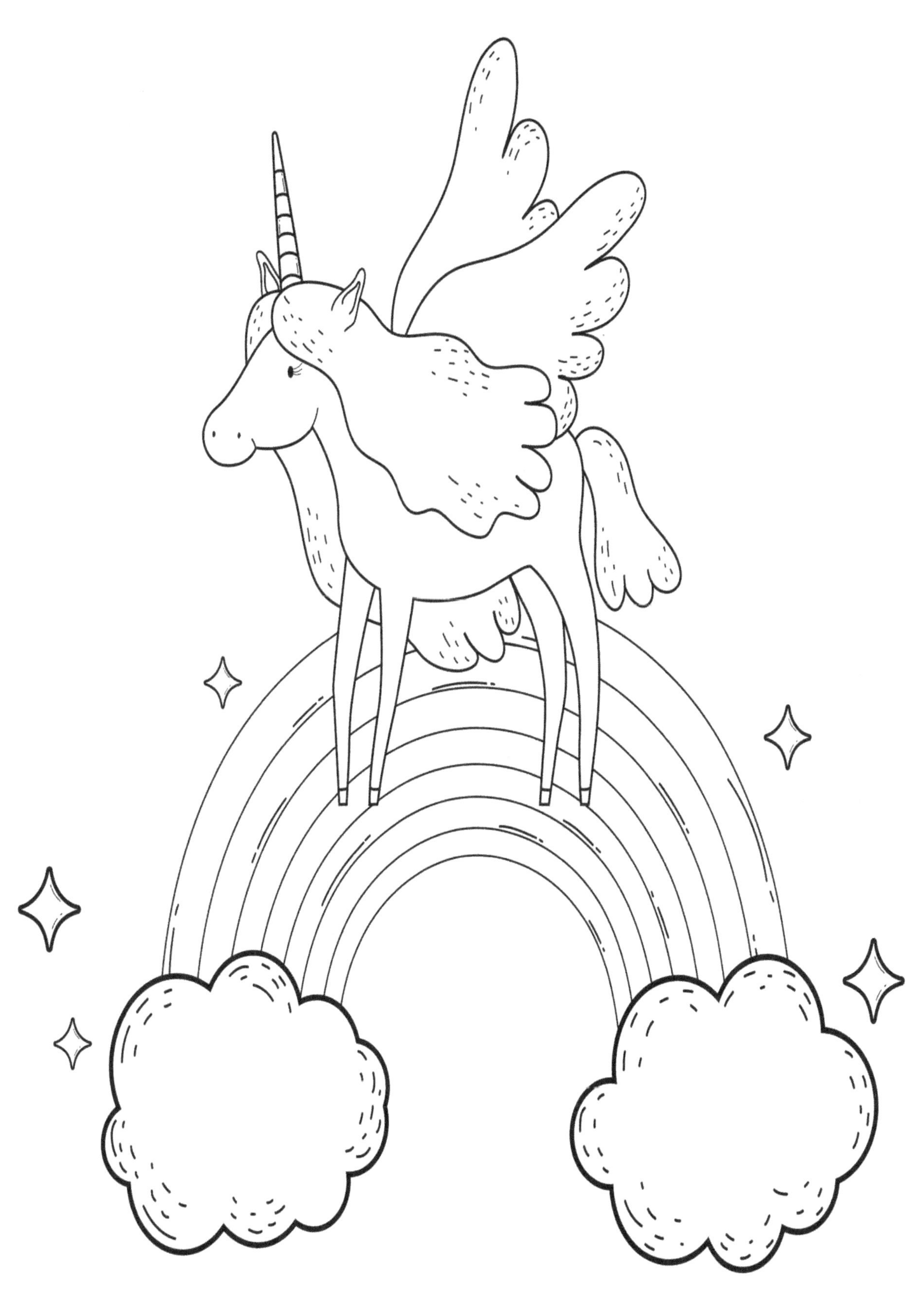

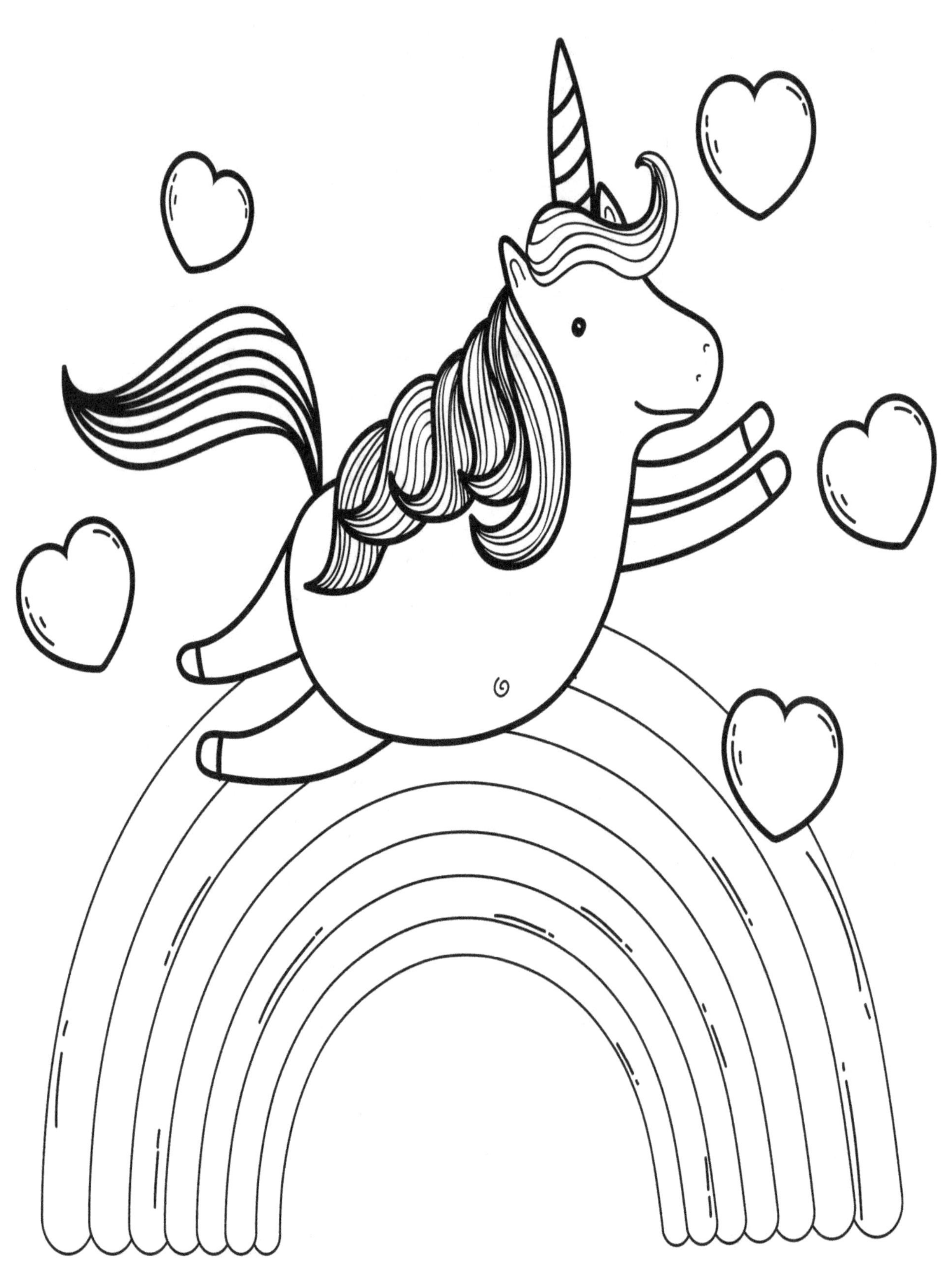

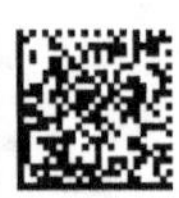

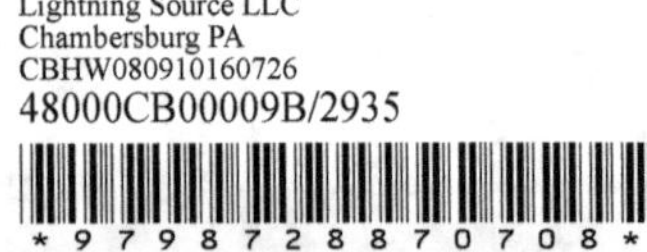
9 798728 870708